MW01181737

INVESTMENT STRATEGIES
for TORTOISES

*Strategies to Manage Your Own Money or Work
with a Financial Advisor More Effectively*

ROBERT G. KAHL
CFA, CPA, MBA

Copyright © 2017 Robert G. Kahl
All rights reserved
First Edition

PAGE PUBLISHING, INC.
New York, NY

First originally published by Page Publishing, Inc. 2017

ISBN 978-1-68409-268-0 (Paperback)
ISBN 978-1-68409-269-7 (Digital)

Printed in the United States of America

CONTENTS

EQUATIONS, FIGURES, AND TABLES

ACKNOWLEDGEMENTS

During the Tucson Book Festival of March 2015, I heard John Vaillant speak at one of the workshops. He is the author of *The Tiger, The Golden Spruce, The Jaguar's Children*, and other publications. There were several people in the audience who had read his books and they gave him very enthusiastic endorsements. After his talk, I bought his book, *The Tiger*, and walked up to the table where he was signing them for readers. He asked if I was an author too as there were many at the book festival and I replied, "No, but I was thinking about it." I didn't realize what he had written at the table until I got home. When I looked inside the front cover, it said, "Bob, you know the way." With that bit of encouragement, my thought project of writing a book became a real project. I appreciate his simple but gentle push to get started as an author. If you take the time to read one of John's books, you won't be disappointed.

I also want to thank Anne Roediger. Anne is a CPA here in Tucson. I had e-mailed a PDF draft of my book to her and her partner. When I had lunch with them a month later, to my surprise, Anne had read the book with a critical eye for detail and provided me with several suggestions for some changes to the book. She provided the finishing touches.

INTRODUCTION

An investment in knowledge always pays the best interest.

Benjamin Franklin

I'm now entering my fourth professional decade managing money. And one thing I've learned is that there's no shortage of surprises. What should happen, doesn't always. What could happen comes to pass instead. And sometimes, what can't happen actually does. Investing, like life, is imminently unpredictable. There are surprises— some good, some bad.

Steve Romick,
portfolio manager of the FPA Crescent Fund

The purpose of this book is to enable nonprofessional investors to make better, informed decisions about investment funds and asset allocation. It should be useful whether you are managing your own money or working with a financial advisor. If you are working with a financial advisor, the content of this book should lead to better, informed discussions and a more active role as a client in establishing investment strategy.

In today's investment world, there are many low-cost, broadly diversified mutual funds, exchange-traded funds, and closed-end funds for different asset classes. But what is the appropriate mix for you? Should you use an active portfolio manager, passive manager that attempts to match the performance of a given index, or a combination of both?

I cover a broad range of investment topics. Entire books have been written about the subject matter of each chapter. I have minimized the use of formulas and attempt to keep it simple but information-rich. There are references at the end of each chapter if you are seeking additional information regarding the subject matter of a chapter.

This book is not designed to teach security analysis or the selection of individual companies for investment. The vast majority of people do not have the time or dedication to select individual securities on their own in a manner that will lead to investment results superior to a broadly diversified fund over a long period of time.

There are times when sensible investment strategies may not work as expected and people may be inclined to abandon them for strategies that have had better results in the recent past. However, sensible strategies are more likely to offer better results over a longer time horizon.

Robert G. Kahl
CFA, CPA, MBA
September 2016

CHAPTER 1

Wishful Thinking Is Not an Investment Strategy

Know thyself.

—Inscription at the Temple
of Apollo at Delphi

Great investors are not unemotional, but are inversely emotional—they get worried when the market is up and feel good when everyone is worried.

—Bill Miller, portfolio manager at
Legg Mason Capital Management

Basis for Decision-Making

A field of study known as behavioral finance has received more attention in recent decades. It seeks to explain why investors often act irrationally and against their own best interests.

What is the basis for your investment decisions? Do you know? Is it a decision process that is supported by research? Are you modeling the investment behavior of successful investors? Below are some common behavioral errors that investors commit. Recognizing the nature of these types of errors is the first step to avoiding them.

Overconfidence—How Smart Are You? No, Really!

According to a *Washington Post* poll, 94% of Americans said they are "above average" in honesty, 89% "above average" in common sense, 86% "above average" in intelligence, and 79% "above average" in looks.

The lack of objectivity among at least some investors leads to overconfidence, which can result in poor decision-making. Overconfidence regarding investments can easily lead to lack of diversification, attempting to time the market, and ignoring information that is contrary to a person's beliefs. Also, some people may be very knowledgeable and capable of making intelligent decisions about particular subjects but their knowledge and intelligence may be more limited when it comes to the subject of investing. Knowing the limitations of your investment knowledge can improve your financial future.

Holding Out for "Top Dollar"

Some investors will hold on to a large position that has gone up in value because they are reluctant to sell a stock that they think may go higher. They are often asking the wrong question. They ask questions such as "How high will it go?" Instead, they should be asking, "How large should the position be given the current potential reward and risk?" Usually, a stock that has gone up much faster than the rest of your portfolio will be a much larger position of your portfolio in percentage terms than it once was, but it most likely will not have the same upside potential that it did in the past.

Holding out for top dollar on an asset that has experienced rapid price appreciation will also lead to a lack of diversification.

Lack of Diversification

A concentrated investment position has worked well for a few billionaires, such as Warren Buffett and Bill Gates, but generally it is not a good idea. For most investors, a lack of diversification increases the probability that they will not meet their goal of a comfortable retirement. It may also increase the probability of achieving better-than-normal returns over a short period of time because the volatility of returns is higher for a less diversified portfolio. Over a longer period of time, however, the probability of higher returns due to volatility will diminish.

Sometimes investors feel that they have a better understanding of one asset class or one company, while they lack such an understanding of other asset classes and companies. Peter Lynch was an advocate of investing in what you know. Nevertheless, the mutual fund that he managed was broadly diversified. If you want to invest in what you know best and can only come up with one or two ideas, you need to expand your horizons.

Market Timing

While it is certainly appealing to think that we can time the market and make dramatic changes in our investment portfolios a few days or weeks in advance of cyclical changes in order to achieve optimal results, the probability of doing so successfully is very small.

The CAPE ratio discussed in a later chapter is not a short-term market timing tool. It is a tool designed to lower the equity allocation of an investment portfolio when potential equity returns are lower and raise the equity allocation when potential equity returns are higher. The goal of using the CAPE ratio for asset allocation is to reduce the potential drawdowns while maintaining a relatively high return over a long time horizon.

Recency Bias

Recency bias is the tendency to think that trends and patterns that we observe in the recent past will continue in the future. It's difficult to deal with uncertainty. There is a plethora of variables that may be relevant to discerning future outcomes. Adopting a recency bias is a simple way of dealing with complexity. It simplifies the decision process by assuming that current trends will continue. They often don't.

Sunk Costs

Sunk costs are historical costs that are irrelevant to current decisions. If an investment has declined in value since its acquisition, some investors may be reluctant to sell until the stock recovers and they can at least "break even." A better course of action is to reevaluate the investment anew and decide if it should be held at this point in time. Normally, the original cost should not be a major consideration when a position has an unrealized loss.

Conclusion

There are some common behavioral errors among investors. A disciplined investment strategy and awareness of these common behavioral errors are likely to improve investment results.

References

Investopedia. www.investopedia.com

Morningstar Investing Classroom—Course 407: Psychology and Investing. http://news.morningstar.com/classroom2/course.asp?docId=145104&page=1&CN=sample

Peterson, Richard L. *Inside the Investor's Brain: The Power of Mind over Money.* John Wiley & Sons, Inc. 2007.

CHAPTER 2

Long-Term Rewards

When I worked at Microsoft, I learned an important lesson about predicting the future. Often, we
expect too much too quickly, but we don't expect
enough over the long-term. Change doesn't happen on schedule, but it can be more sweeping
than anybody imagined.
                    —Bill Gates, co-founder of Microsoft

Move only when you have an advantage.
                              —Charles Munger,
                    vice chairman of Berkshire Hathaway

What's Your Time Horizon?

Investors should determine their time horizon based upon projected
income, cash expenditures, health status, and other considerations.
Investors who have a relatively short time horizon (one to five years)
should normally have an asset allocation that reduces volatility.
Investors who have a relatively long time horizon (more than ten
years) should normally have a higher allocation to investments with
higher expected returns, which are normally accompanied by higher
levels of volatility.

From a behavioral standpoint, the time horizon of many investors becomes much shorter during market declines. That should not be the case. Investors' time horizons should not change based upon market performance.

Risk Tolerance

Many investors are unrealistic about their risk tolerance. When the market is going higher, they think they have a high risk tolerance. When the market declines, they suddenly decide that they have a low tolerance for risk and sell when valuation levels may actually be very attractive.

Investors should consider the historical volatility and the probabilities of the range of potential outcomes of their investment holdings.

The Trade-Off

Money is normally defined as a currency that is accepted as payment for goods and services and repayment of debts in a particular country. While gold and silver have been used as money in the past, they are now generally considered to be alternative but globally accepted currencies that must be exchanged for a fiat currency to be used for payments.

People often refer to investments in stocks and bonds as "money." This use of the term is incorrect. Investors may think of common stocks and fixed-income securities as money because there is almost always some bid available. Their securities can be sold, and cash is available after a three-day settlement period. However, the price of common stocks and fixed-income securities may fluctuate considerably, unlike "money."

People don't refer to real estate as money because it is widely acknowledged that the time for an acceptable offer to emerge on a property is very difficult to predict.

Common stocks represent a proportional interest in a business. People buy common stocks in exchange for money because they expect a combination of dividend income, dividend reinvestment, and price appreciation to give them more purchasing power in the future. Price appreciation or depreciation is the result of earnings growth or contraction and changes in valuation. Valuation is the price that investors are willing to pay based on some metric, such as the price-to-earnings ratio.

Fixed-income investments generally offer a fixed-income payment and a return of the original principal amount. There are variations of fixed-income securities that have variable interest rates or step-up rates, but both types of securities return the original principal amount at maturity.

Treasury Inflation-Protected Securities (TIPS) normally fall into the category of fixed income securities, although both principal and interest payments will increase or decrease based upon the consumer price index.

The chart below illustrates the volatility of returns for different holding periods of US small capitalization stocks (Ibbotson Small Company Stock Index), US large capitalization stocks (S&P 500 Index), US government bonds (twenty-year US Treasury bond), and US Treasury bills. The volatility of returns is high for one year holdings periods, especially small-cap stocks. The range of annualized return outcomes narrows substantially as you extend the holding period. Most people do not think in terms of a twenty-year holding period, but if they did, they would probably find the risk-to-return trade-off to be acceptable.

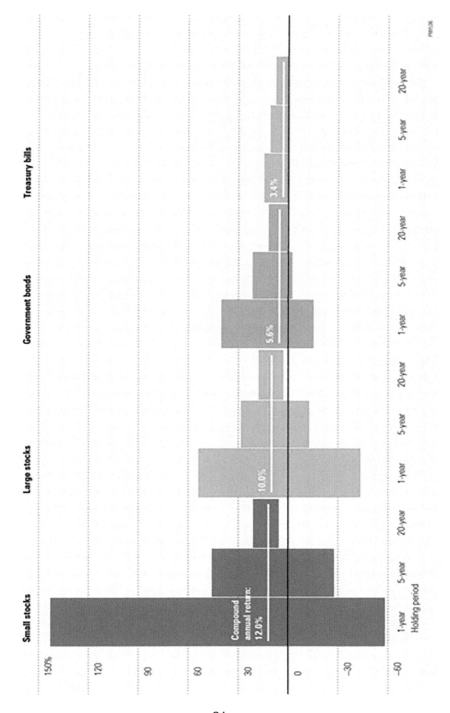

Figure 2-1 Holding Periods and Volatility 1926-2015

LONG-TERM REWARDS

Source: Morningstar.

21

Mutual Fund Flows—What They Say about Average Investors

DALBAR's Quantitative Analysis of Investor Behavior has been published annually for over fifteen years and measures the effects of investor decisions to buy, sell, and switch into and out of mutual funds. Their results have shown that the average investor earns significantly less than the mutual funds they own due to poor timing decisions. For twenty-year rolling periods from 1998 to 2013, they estimated that the average equity fund investor had annualized returns that varied between 4 and 11% below the S&P 500 Index. Morningstar has conducted similar studies and had similar results.

Investors often talk jokingly about a strategy of "buy low and sell high," but most investors do just the opposite. Analysis of mutual fund flows is consistent with the DALBAR and Morningstar studies. Net withdrawals from mutual funds are high when markets decline to some extent because the withdrawals contribute to forced selling by mutual funds. Net purchases of mutual funds are high when the market has been going up.

During the financial crisis of 2008–2009, some investors sold near the bottom of the market because they "didn't want to lose any more money." Some of these same investors later reestablished equity positions at higher prices because "everyone is making money but me." Use of the CAPE ratio described in a chapter later in this book is a strategy supported by empirical evidence to reduce risk when valuation levels are high (and expected returns are low) and increase potential returns when valuation levels are low (and expected returns are high).

Conclusion

Investors should be realistic about their time horizon, tolerance for risk, and (in)ability to time turns in the financial markets. Poor market timing decisions by many mutual fund investors contribute to substantial underperformance relative to the mutual funds that they purchase.

References

Jing, Chong Ser. "The Most Important Chart Investors Have to See in the Bear Market Now." Motley Fool, September 30, 2015. https://www.fool.sg/2015/09/30/the-most-important-chart-investors-have-to-see-in-the-bear-market-now/

DALBAR Quantitative Analysis of Investor Behavior. http://www.dalbar.com/Portals/dalbar/cache/News/PressReleases/2014QAIBHighlightsPR.pdf

Hsu, Jason. "If Factor Returns Are Predictable, Why Is There an Investor Return Gap?" http://www.researchaffiliates.com/Our%20Ideas/Insights/Fundamentals/Pages/488_If_Factor_Returns_Are_Predictable_Why_Is_There_an_Investor_Return_Gap.aspx

CHAPTER 3

Pick Your Poison (or Risk)

Take calculated risks. That is quite different from being rash.

—General George Patton

Investment Risk Is Unavoidable

Since the midnineteenth century, *poison* has been slang for alcoholic drink. This was derived from the Latin root *toxicum* (poison) of the word *intoxicate*. Thus, the phrases "Pick your poison" and "What's your poison?" arose in drinking establishments. While the risks of intoxication can be avoided if one doesn't drink alcoholic beverages, there will always be some type of risk associated with investments.

Many people would like to live in a risk-free world, but it doesn't really exist. Some investors may think they are not taking any risk by focusing on one type of risk while ignoring others. There are risks associated with all investments, even so-called "risk-free" assets such as US Treasury securities or FDIC-insured bank accounts.

Let's Define Risk

There are a few different definitions of risk that are commonly used in the context of investments. FINRA (Financial Industry

Regulatory Authority) defines risk as any uncertainty with respect to your investments that has the potential to negatively affect your financial welfare. Higher risk of a particular investment or asset class is normally associated with higher rewards. The discussion below will describe many types of investment risk associated with equities and fixed income.

Some investment professionals define risk as the permanent loss of capital. The assumption is that negative price movements are often temporary in nature and asset prices eventually recover. This raises two questions:

1. How does one know that a price decline is only temporary and not permanent in nature?
2. If a price decline is temporary in nature, will the price recover before the investor must sell in order to meet a cash expenditure requirement?

If an investment must be sold before the price recovers, then a temporary price decline will result in a permanent loss of capital. Thus, it is important for investors to make projections of their future cash flows and to consider the volatility of their prospective investment returns before they establish their investment allocation.

Other investment professionals define risk in terms of the standard deviation of historical returns of a specific investment. Historical returns are used as a basis for the calculation because we don't know what future returns will be. Thus, this type of calculation of risk will vary over time.

Do "Risk-Free" Assets Really Exist?

In the United States, we often refer to US Treasury and Agency securities and FDIC-insured bank accounts as risk-free assets. However, there are some risks associated with these investments that you may not have considered.

While most would consider the *risk of default* by the US Treasury to be insignificant, there is some risk of default. On several occasions, Congress has vigorously debated the debt-ceiling authorization and has always chosen to raise the debt ceiling rather than cut back federal government spending and balance the budget. However, if Congress does not raise the debt ceiling and extraordinary budget measures are exhausted, the US government would be legally unable to borrow. And if cash on hand were inadequate, it would default on its debt. Or suppose that Congress continued to raise the debt ceiling and the US government debt-to-GDP ratio continued to rise, while the Federal Reserve Banks bought all US Treasury debt that investors were not willing to buy in order to avoid a failed Treasury auction. This process would expand the money supply and lower the central bank's capital-to-assets ratio, eventually raising the risk of currency devaluation or insolvency of the central bank.

FDIC-insured bank accounts are normally considered to be risk-free. Since the FDIC was established in 1933, no depositor has lost a penny of FDIC-insured funds. At the end of 2009, the FDIC was responsible for insuring $5.4 trillion of bank deposits, and it closed the year with a *negative* fund balance of $20.8 billion. At the end of two successive years (2009–2010), the FDIC had a negative fund balance, and Congress did not authorize any additional funds to improve the FDIC's capital position. By the end of 2011, the FDIC's fund balance had improved to a positive $11.8 billion, which covered $7.0 trillion of insured deposits. Thus, the ratio of the insurance fund balance to insured deposits was still remarkably low at 0.17% at the end of 2011.

Risk Associated with Equities

There are a variety of risks associated with investments in common stocks, convertible bonds, convertible preferred stocks, and other equity vehicles (real estate investment trusts, master limited partnerships, etc.). Since preferred stocks usually have a fixed periodic payment without a conversion feature, we will include them in the fixed-income category in this discussion. Some of the different types of risk associated with equities are the following:

- *Operating risk of the business.* Generally, dividend payments from a business depend on cash flow generated from the business less capital expenditures. Employees, landlords, and debt holders among others, must be paid before shareholders can be paid dividends. If a company experiences revenue declines and/or is unable to maintain profit margins, cash flow from the business may decline, and dividends may be reduced. This is often accompanied by a decline in the company's share price. This type of risk associated with a single company, however, can be reduced through diversification.
- *Financial risk of the business.* If a company is financed with debt and highly leveraged, it is more susceptible to a default on its debt, which could result in a total loss to its common stock investors. Like operating risk, this type of risk can be reduced through diversification.
- *Economic recessions and depressions.* This type of operational risk is systemic in nature and cannot be avoided through diversification. During the last financial crisis, real GDP declined by –0.3%, measured from calendar year 2007 to 2008. S&P 500 reported earnings (inflation adjusted, measured in constant August 2015 US dollars) declined 77.5% during this same period, from $75.09 for calendar year 2007 to $16.87 in 2008. Corporate earnings are highly correlated with GDP but much more volatile.

Risk Associated with Fixed Income

There are a number of risks associated with fixed-income securities. Among them are the following:

- *Credit (or default) risk.* There is a possibility that a fixed-income security will default and be unable to meet its contractual commitment to make principal and interest payments as scheduled.

- *Credit spread risk.* A fixed-income security may experience a price decline due to credit concerns without actually defaulting. Credit spread refers to the additional yield in excess of the yield on a "risk-free" fixed-income security with a similar maturity. Credit spreads change over time, depending upon prospective default rates of individual bonds or bonds with similar credit ratings.

- *Interest rate risk.* When interest rates rise, the discounted value of scheduled principal and interest payments declines. The extent of any price decline will depend on the duration of a fixed-income security. Duration is the weighted average term to maturity of all interest and principal payments. Option-adjusted duration is duration adjusted for the first call or put provision. Interest rate risk can be reduced by investing in shorter-term fixed-income securities, but doing so will increase reinvestment risk, and some price appreciation from lower interest rates will be foregone.

- *Negative convexity.* This isn't so much a risk as a feature of certain types of bonds that may already be reflected in the price of the bond. As interest rates change, the duration of some bonds will change in a manner contrary to the best interests of the bondholder. When interest rates fall, bonds with call features are more likely to be called, shortening the duration. When interest rates rise, they are less likely to be called, which lengthens the duration.

- Mortgage-backed securities (MBS) and preferred shares act in this manner as well. When interest rates fall, mortgages are more likely to be refinanced and MBS receive more principal payments. Preferred shares are often perpetual in nature and have no maturity date. They do, however, have redemption features so the issuer may refinance and redeem the preferred shares (at par value or a small premium to par value) when it is to their advantage.

- *Inflation risk.* The coupon rate when a bond is first issued will reflect the inflation expectation at the time of issuance. If the inflation rate increases significantly from the time of issuance, market rates of interest will increase. This is especially detrimental to holders of longer-term bonds. The market price of longer-term bonds will decline more because the present value of a bond is calculated by discounting all future principal and interest payments based on current interest rates. There are some fixed income securities such as Treasury Inflation-Protected Securities (TIPS) that have payments that adjust on the basis of the inflation rate. Common stocks also offer some protection against inflation.

- *Reinvestment risk.* This is one type of risk that is often ignored. Interest rates may decline, and principal and interest payments that are received will have to be invested at lower interest rates when reinvested in other fixed-income securities. This type of risk can be reduced by investing in longer-term bonds, but doing so will increase interest rate risk.

Risks Associated with Both Equities and Fixed Income

Some of the risks associated with both equities and fixed income are the following:

- *Market risk.* There is some price volatility inherent in virtually all investments. Market risk refers to any decline in market value that may or may not be related to economic or business fundamentals.

- *Currency risk.* People have a home bias—a preference for investments within their own country. This is a natural bias. In the United States, this is a risk that many people do not consider because we have not had a major devaluation or hyperinflation in our lifetime. However, we should not assume that currency stability is an immutable fact.

- *Liquidity risk.* Some assets are not as easily sold as others. Less marketable investment securities typically have a wider bid-to-ask spread. If the position being acquired or sold is relatively large compared to the average trading volume or existing bid-to-ask order size, the order execution will likely have a negative impact on the price.
- *Mortality risk.* Some investments such as pensions or annuities that pay only as long as you are alive may run the risk of not recovering your original investment.
- *Opportunity cost risk.* We don't usually think of missing an opportunity as risk, but maybe we should.
- *Political risk.* The political environment of a country may change in a number of ways: political leadership, tax policies, administrative policies, legislation, and judicial decisions.
- *Wars and natural disasters.* These are risks that we do not like to consider, but they happen. Insurance policies usually exclude wars and natural disasters from coverage because damage is so widespread.
- *Investment structure risk.* Some investment structures require additional due diligence before a decision is made regarding their purchase. Generally, closed-end funds should not be purchased at a premium or small discount to net asset value because there is some probability that they may eventually sell at a larger discount to net asset value. Some closed-end funds and ETFs may be structured with a leverage feature that may increase the volatility of returns. Some hedge funds lack adequate separation of duties and the involvement of independent third parties to prevent fraud.
- *Manager risk.* Poor security selection by an investment manager may cause a fund or portfolio to underperform relevant benchmarks or other funds with a similar investment objective.

The purpose of discussing the various types of risk is to develop a better understanding of the nature of various investment risks and reduce the probability of overreacting to inevitable declines in the financial markets.

Conclusion

Investment risk is unavoidable. A comprehensive awareness of risk as well as potential reward will likely lead to better investment returns and avoidance of emotional responses to negative price action.

References

For historical information regarding the Shiller PE ratio, S&P 500 and US Treasury yields, see http://www.multpl.com/

Federal Reserve Bank of St. Louis, Economic Research Department. https://research.stlouisfed.org/fred2/

"The Reality of Investment Risk." FINRA. http://www.finra.org/investors/reality-investment-risk

CHAPTER 4

Asset Pricing Theories and Factors

I'm a firm believer that to really understand a business takes years, not months. As an investment analyst you think you understand a business from the outside, but the reality is that, once you are inside, you can go on learning for five or ten years.

—Chris Corrigan,
Australian businessman and
former managing director
of the Patrick Corporation

Efficient Market Hypothesis (EMH)

Proponents of the efficient market hypothesis (EMH) state that the market is efficient and that security prices reflect all available information. There are three versions of the EMH: weak, semi-strong, and strong. The weak form asserts that all public trading data is reflected in security pricing and charting analysis is futile. The semi-strong form asserts that all publicly available information is reflected in security prices and charting or fundamental analysis is futile. The strong form states that all information, both public and private, is reflected in security prices and consequently, even insider information cannot be used successfully to achieve excess returns.

Capital Asset Pricing Model (CAPM)

In the early 1960s, William Sharpe, John Lintner, and Jan Mossin developed the capital asset pricing model (CAPM) in published articles that built on the work of Harry Markowitz. CAPM is a theoretical construct that starts with a set of simplifying assumptions. All investors have a homogenous set of beliefs regarding investment strategy, time horizon, and other considerations, with the exception of initial wealth and risk tolerance. All efficient portfolios (in terms of the ratio of expected return to potential volatility) will be some combination of the risk-free asset (RF) and the market portfolio (M), which includes all traded risky assets. The allocation between RF and M will depend on an investor's risk tolerance.

The expected return of any individual asset will be a function of the expected return of the risk-free asset, the expected return of the market (M), and the beta coefficient, which measures the tendency of a security's price to move with the market.

Equation 4-1 Capital Asset Pricing Model

$$E(A) = RF + b(E(M) - RF)$$

Where

$E(A)$ = expected return of the asset

$E(M)$ = expected return of the market

RF = risk-free asset return

b = beta coefficient or sensitivity of the expected asset return to the market return

A beta coefficient of 1 would mean the asset is expected to move with the market, have the same volatility and the same expected return. A beta coefficient greater than 1 would mean the stock is more volatile than the market and would have a higher expected return. A negative beta coefficient would mean the stock is expected to move contrary to the market and have a lower expected return than the RF asset. Companies with higher beta coefficients will have higher costs of capital because investors will require higher expected returns for the additional risk.

Arbitrage Pricing Theory (APT)

In a series of academic articles published in 1971 through 1976, Stephen Ross offered an alternative to CAPM called the arbitrage pricing theory (APT) of capital assets. Assets may deviate from fair value, but they are quickly repriced due to arbitrage—undervalued securities are purchased and overvalued securities are sold short to restore equilibrium to the market. Assets are priced according to a factor structure with different risk premiums for different macro-economic factors and different exposure or sensitivity for specific assets to those factors. APT does not identify or define the number of important factors. That task was left for future researchers.

While APT focused on macroeconomic factors, the term *factor* now commonly refers to any characteristic of a group of securities that is useful in explaining expected return and risk.

Fama–French Three-Factor Model

Eugene Fama of the Booth School of Business, University of Chicago, and Kenneth French of the Amos Tuck School of Business, Dartmouth College, are finance professors that collaborated on several studies. They are both consultants to, board members of, and shareholders in Dimensional Fund Advisors (DFA), which implements their factor models and had $381 billion in assets under management as of December 2014. Outside of DFA, their studies have been very influential in the professional investment community.

In June 1992, Eugene Fama and Kenneth French introduced a three-factor model that isolated the effects of two easily measured variables—size (market capitalization) and book-to-market equity. After adjusting for size and book-to-market equity, they considered the explanatory power of beta. Their conclusion: "In a nutshell, market beta seems to have no role in explaining the average returns on NYSE, AMEX, and NASDAQ stocks for 1963–1990, while size and book-to-market equity capture the cross-sectional variation in average stock returns that is related to leverage and Earnings/Price." Fama and French found that companies with higher book-to-market equity ratios (or lower price-to-book value ratios) had higher returns. They also found that average returns decrease with size; smaller companies had higher returns.

How Many Factors Are There?

Investment strategies based upon factor models are often called *smart beta* strategies. In contrast to a market capitalization weighted index fund, a factor or *smart beta* approach constructs portfolios based upon rules to capture certain investment factors. The goal is to improve risk-adjusted returns relative to capitalization-weighted indices.

Factor models have been tested extensively to identify systematic sources of excess return. Some factors are risk-related, while others are related to investor behavior. Jason Hsu and his associates at Research Affiliates in Newport Beach published an article titled "A Framework for Assessing Factors and Implementing Smart Beta Strategies." They reviewed the financial literature and found that more than 250 "supposed" factors have been tested. They proposed a framework for identifying investable factors that can be incorporated into strategies that will produce reliable positive premium returns in the future. They write:

> For a factor to be considered robust, it must be based on a meaningful economic intuition, be supported by deep empirical literature, be robust across timespans and geographies, and deliver excess returns despite minor changes in definition. For a factor to be considered passively implementable, it must deliver excess returns in liquid names, require only infrequent trading and low turnover, and have the capacity to accom-

modate very large in- and outflows. Otherwise, highly skilled (and thus more costly) active trading would be required for effectively capturing the premium.

Hsu et al. do not recommend specific factors but instead discuss many of the considerations regarding the selection and allocation to factor strategies. They conclude that the appropriate factor allocation will be highly dependent on the investor's definition of risk, risk tolerance, ability to implement tactical/dynamic allocation, and the governance structure and politics at an organization. They also note that factor "expected returns and correlations can be time-varying and are often mean-reverting," so heavy reliance on recent data might be misleading for asset allocation decisions.

Morningstar is used as a resource by many investors. Their "style box" uses the value/growth and size factors to describe the makeup of various fund portfolios. Chapters 5 and 6 of this book will have a more detailed discussion about strategies based upon value and market capitalization strategies.

The remainder of this chapter will describe some of the more common factors used for security selection. Some factors that can be considered alternative definitions will be grouped together.

Value

The value factor is probably the most common factor used in investment factor models to provide excess returns over longer time periods. For the purpose of investment style descriptions and the development of factor investment models, the distinction between value and growth stocks is now usually based on rankings using ratios of price-to-book value or price-to-earnings. When a database of stocks is ranked from highest to lowest, the stocks with the lowest price-to-book value or lowest price-to-earnings ratio are considered to be value stocks. Stocks with the highest ratios are considered to be growth stocks. Some alternative criteria for defining value and growth stocks in the financial studies are price-to-cash flow, price-to-free cash flow, or price-to-sales.

Several studies over relatively long periods of time indicate that value stocks outperform their universe of stocks. However, there are periods of time when the value factor does not perform as well as growth stocks. The next chapter will go into some detail regarding studies on value versus growth.

Market Capitalization and Liquidity

Low size or smaller capitalization companies have had higher total returns in the past according to some studies. Smaller companies tend to have narrower product or service offerings and less access to capital than larger companies that may be more established. Thus, the higher returns are thought to be associated with higher risk of the business operations.

Smaller companies are also generally less liquid or more difficult to buy or sell in size without impacting the price. Some researchers consider market capitalization and liquidity to be distinct factors, but companies grouped on the basis of these factors are likely to have similar characteristics.

Dividend Yield

Some investment portfolios are designed to have a higher dividend yield. Dividend yield is sometimes considered a proxy for value because stocks with higher dividend yields tend to be more mature companies with lower growth rates and higher dividend payouts. Investment funds designed as value funds often have characteristics that are similar to funds designed for higher dividend yields.

Gregg Fisher used multivariate analysis to study the source of higher returns from high dividend yield stocks. He examined US stocks during the period of August 1, 1979 to July 31, 2012. His conclusion:

> First, by focusing on high-yield-dividend stocks, investors unwittingly tilted their portfolios to value stocks. The dividend yield factor is subsumed in the value and earnings yield factors. Second, the value factor, not the yield factor, was responsible for the excess performance over the period studied. And finally, the dividend yield factor tilt also brought with it a high exposure to the earnings yield factor, which is a commonly used method for identifying value stocks and a strong contributor to positive returns.

Shareholder Yield

Mebane Faber, who is a cofounder and chief investment officer of Cambria Investment Management, is an advocate of using shareholder yield in the stock selection process. In his book *Shareholder Yield: A Better Approach to Yield Investing*, he defines shareholder yield as follows:

$$\text{(dividends + net share buybacks + net debt pay down) / market capitalization}$$

Although share buybacks and debt pay downs do not put cash in shareholders' accounts, they benefit shareholders indirectly. Faber's firm sponsors two ETFs that screen for high shareholder yield: Cambria Shareholder Yield ETF (SYLD) and Cambria Foreign Shareholder Yield ETF (FYLD).

Momentum

Momentum factor investing is a strategy that involves investing in companies that have performed well in the recent past. This is generally considered to be a riskier strategy than others as it relies on the herding behavior and recency bias of others rather than fundamentals. Some investment managers combine momentum with fundamental factors. Some investment managers choose not to incorporate momentum into their strategies due to its apparent lack of intuitive economic rationale and higher expected trading costs.

Profitability

In September 2014, Fama and French published a working paper to describe the results of their work on a five-factor model. The five factors included in their model are as follows: beta, size, value, profitability (as measured by return on equity), and investment patterns (as measured by change in total assets). They found that profitability and investment resulted in higher returns. The profitability factor has since been incorporated into some factor-based fund strategies, although there is still some controversy about it.

Low Volatility

There is evidence from several studies that low-volatility stocks have achieved higher returns. This is contrary to what most investors would expect as volatility is a measure of risk.

Larry Swedroe, director of research for the BAM Alliance, believes that much of this advantage has since disappeared. He cites a study that concluded that low-volatility strategies outperformed their corresponding capitalization-weighted market indexes due to exposure to the value factor. He examined the two largest low-volatility ETFs: the PowerShares S&P 500 Low Volatility Portfolio (SPLV) and the iShares MSCI USA Minimum Volatility ETF (USMV). Swedroe found that both ETFs had higher valuations than either the Russell 1000 or the Russell 1000 Value indices. As a result, he concluded that SPLV and USMV were not likely to provide higher returns in the future because they no longer had significant exposure to the value factor.

Quality

There is no agreement in the financial literature regarding what constitutes a quality company. Some of the factors related to quality in the financial literature include profit margins, growth in profitability, financial leverage, earnings stability, accounting quality, and expense levels that should lead to future growth (such as research and development and advertising).

Kalesnik and Kose (2014) at Research Affiliates are skeptical that a quality factor on its own is a good investment approach. They believe, however, that the academic research supports using qualitative measures in addition to the value factor to make better portfolios.

Tactical Considerations

In an article published in February 2016 by Rob Arnott and his associates at Research Affiliates, "How Smart Beta Can Go Wrong," the authors recommend caution in the assessment of factor selection. They analyze the composition of returns to identify the portion of returns due to changes in relative valuations. In the following excerpt, *alpha* refers to portfolio returns in excess of what a pricing model (CAPM, APT, or three-factor model) would predict. They write:

> Value-add can be structural (hence, plausibly a source of future alpha) or situational (a consequence of rising enthusiasm for, and valuation of, the selected factor or strategy). Few, *if any*, of the research papers in support of newly identified factors make any effort to determine whether rising valuations contributed to the lofty historical returns. The unsurprising reality is that many of the new factors deliver alpha only because they've grown more expensive—absent rising relative valuations, there's nothing left!

> Today, only the value category shows some degree of relative cheapness, precisely because its recent

performance has been weak! Generally speaking, normal factor returns, net of changes in valuation levels, are much lower than recent returns suggest. Investors entering the space should adjust their expectations accordingly.

Conclusion

There are a variety of asset pricing models that differ in terms of complexity and theoretical basis. Some of the more popular asset pricing models are the capital asset pricing model (CAPM), arbitrage pricing theory (APT), three-factor model, and five-factor model. During the last two decades, investing on the basis of factors in order to capture excess returns has become more popular. Investor expectations for future returns on the basis of factors should consider the impact of changes in relative valuation levels.

References

Wikipedia. www.wikipedia.com

Arnott, Rob, Noah Beck, Vitali Kalesnik, and John West. "How Can 'Smart Beta' Go Horribly Wrong?" Research Affiliates Fundamentals, February 2016. https://www.researchaffiliates.com/Our%20Ideas/Insights/Fundamentals/Pages/442_How_Can_Smart_Beta_Go_Horribly_Wrong.aspx

Bender, Jennifer, Remy Briand, Dimitris Melas, and Raman Aylur Subramanian. "Foundations of Factor Investing." MSCI Research Insight, December 2013. https://www.msci.com/resources/pdfs/Foundations_of_Factor_Investing.pdf

Blitz, D. and P. van Vliet. 2007. "The Volatility Effect: Lower Risk without Lower Return." Journal of Portfolio Management, Fall 2007, Vol. 34, No. 1: pp. 102–113. http://www.robeco.com/images/the-volatility-effect-lower-risk-without-lower-return.pdf

Bodie, Zvi, Alex Kane, and Alan J. Marcus. 1993. *Investments, Second Edition.* Irwin Professional Publishing.

Faber, Mebane. 2013. *Shareholder Yield: A Better Approach to Yield Investing.* Idea Farm, LP.

Fama, Eugene and Kenneth French. "The Cross-Section of Expected Stock Returns." Journal of Finance, Volume 47, Issue 2, June 1992, p. 427–465. http://www.bengrahaminvesting.ca/Research/Papers/French/The_Cross-Section_of_Expected_Stock_Returns.pdf

Fama, Eugene and Kenneth French. "A Five-Factor Asset Pricing Model." Social Science Research Network. Working paper last revised September 23, 2014. http://papers.ssrn.com/sol3/papers.cfm?abstract_id=2287202

Fisher, Gregg S. "Dividend Investing: A Value Tilt in Disguise?" Journal of Financial Planning. https://www.onefpa.org/journal/Pages/Dividend%20Investing%20A%20Value%20Tilt%20in%20Disguise.aspx

Hsu, Jason, Vitali Kalesnik and Vivek Viswanathan. "A Framework for Assessing Factors and Implementing Smart Beta Strategies." The Journal of Index Investing, Summer 2015, Volume 6, Number 1. https://www.researchaffiliates.com/Our%20Ideas/Insights/Papers/Pages/373_A_Framework_for_Assessing_Factors_and_Implementing_Smart_Beta_Strategies.aspx

Kalesnik, Vitali and Engin Kose. "The Moneyball of Quality Investing." Research Affiliates, Fundamentals, June 2014. https://www.researchaffiliates.com/Our%20Ideas/Insights/Fundamentals/Pages/259_The_Moneyball_of_Quality_Investing.aspx

Ross, Stephen A. 1976. "The Arbitrage Theory of Capital Asset Pricing." Journal of Economic Theory 13, p. 341–360, http://down.cenet.org.cn/upfile/36/2009323121657103.pdf

Swedroe, Larry. "Be Wary of the Low Vol Factor." ETF.com, Index Investor Corner, February 13, 2015. http://www.etf.com/sections/index-investor-corner/beware-how-low-vol-anomaly-works?nopaging=1

CHAPTER 5

Value versus Growth Stocks

> Value investing is at its core the marriage of a contrarian streak and a calculator.
> —Seth Klarman, founder of the Baupost Group, a private investment partnership

Benjamin Graham and Value Investing

Benjamin Graham and David Dodd's book, *Security Analysis*, was first published in 1934. The book, along with Graham's teaching at Columbia Business School, had an influence on the budding profession of investment analysis, which had a need for some scholarly discipline at the time. Benjamin Graham's second book, *The Intelligent Investor*, was published in 1949, and subsequent editions followed. Graham's disciples included some well-known investors such as Warren Buffett (a former student and associate of Graham), Charlie Munger, William Ruane, Irving Kahn, Walter Schloss, Jean-Marie Eveillard, and Seth Klarman.

Graham and Dodd's concept of value investing involves buying securities when prices are below their intrinsic value by a margin wide enough to provide a "margin of safety." The estimate of intrinsic value is based upon fundamental analysis, but it has some degree of uncertainty because we are using estimates of future results.

Value and Growth Stocks Today

The distinction between value and growth stocks is defined in a variety of ways in today's financial markets. In the empirical studies, the value and growth categories are based upon a ranking of stocks using a single ratio such as price-to-book value, price-to-earnings, or price-to-free cash flow.

Some information providers use a combination of several variables to characterize a stock. Two of the most prominent data providers are FTSE Russell and Morningstar, so we will examine how they make the distinction between value and growth stocks.

FTSE Russell—Value and Growth Styles

FTSE Russell is a leading provider of benchmarking, analytics, and data solutions for investors. Their indices are used as the basis for a variety of index-linked ETFs sponsored by providers such as BlackRock, Charles Schwab, Direxion, Invesco, JPMorgan, ProShare Advisors, RBC, Vanguard, and others.

Each of FTSE Russell 's US-based indices (Russell 1000®, Russell 2000®, and Russell 3000®) has subindices for value and growth characteristics. FTSE Russell uses one variable to define value: the price-to-book value ratio. Two other variables are used to define growth—the IBES forecast medium-term growth rate (two-year forecast) and sales-per-share historical growth rate (for the most recent five years). Since the criteria for value and growth are not mutually exclusive, stocks may have characteristics of both.

Individual stocks in each of the base indices are scored and ranked on the basis of a composite value score (CVS). The value variable represents 50% of the CVS, and the two growth variables represent the remaining 50% of the score. Stocks are assigned weights in the subindices on the basis of their CVS and are always fully represented by their combination of value and growth weights. Some stocks may have a 100% weight in the value or growth subindex while another stock may have an 80% weight in the value subindex and a 20% weight in the growth subindex. As of January 2016, the Russell 1000 Value Index had 688 stocks and the Russell 1000 Growth Index had 643 stocks, so there are many stocks that have representation in both subindices.

Morningstar—Value and Growth Styles

Morningstar has a process that is different from FTSE Russell to describe the value and growth characteristics of stocks. Individual stocks are scored on the basis of the following variables:

- Value score components and weights
  - Forward looking—price-to-prospective earnings: 50.0%
  - Historical measures
    - Price-to-book value: 12.5%
    - Price-to-sales: 12.5%
    - Price-to-cash flow: 12.5%
    - Dividend yield: 12.5%

- Growth score components and weights
  - Forward looking—long-term projected earnings growth: 50%
  - Historical measures
    - Earnings growth: 12.5%
    - Sales growth: 12.5%
    - Cash flow growth: 12.5%
    - Book value growth: 12.5%

Stocks are scored from 0 to 100 for both value and growth within the same capitalization range. The overall score for a stock is determined by subtracting the value score from the growth score. Overall scores may range from 100 (low dividend yield, extreme growth) to –100 (high yield, low growth). Stocks that fall within the middle of the range are called core holdings. On the growth-value score continuum, approximately one-third of the stocks within a capitalization range are assigned to each style box: growth, value, and core. The style attributes of individual stock holdings are then used to determine the style classification of stock mutual funds.

Evidence from Empirical Studies

Contrary to the efficient market hypothesis, advocates of investment strategies based on factors offer evidence that the financial markets are inefficient and that investors can take advantage of these systematic inefficiencies to generate superior returns.

There have been numerous studies on the subject of value-versus-growth investment strategies. Table 5-1 summarizes nine of the studies on the subject. The studies cover different time periods and different stock universes. Two of the studies include foreign stocks. The Bauman, Conover, and Miller study is the most comprehensive with regard to international stocks and includes 2,800 stocks in twenty-one countries over a time period of ten years.

The most common variables that were tested were price-to-book value (P / BV), price-to-earnings (P/E), and price-to-cash flow (P/CF). Other variables that were tested included earnings growth rates, sales growth rates, and dividend yield. Stocks with a low price relative to book value, earnings, or cash flow were considered to be value stocks, while those with high ratios were considered to be growth stocks. Stocks with high dividend yields were also considered to be value stocks.

The studies utilized similar methodologies with regard to the testing of variables. Table 5-1 shows the types of companies included in the studies, how they were grouped, the frequency of rebalancing, and the variables tested. Stocks in the selected universe for the studies were ranked on the basis of the independent variables to be tested. Portfolios were then formed by grouping stocks on the basis of the rankings. After a certain period of time, stocks were then ranked again, and the portfolios were rebalanced accordingly. The returns on the various portfolios were then compared.

The results of all nine studies were consistent. When value portfolios (stocks with the lowest P/E, P/BV, etc.) were compared to growth portfolios (stocks with the highest P/E, P/BV, etc.), the value portfolios outperformed the growth portfolios in all nine studies. The value portfolios were also compared to a benchmark index in six of the nine studies and outperformed the benchmark in all six studies. This held true for all of the variables in the various studies that were used to identify value stocks. Several studies compared investment returns after different time periods. For purposes of comparison in Table 5-1, all differences in investment performance returns are shown on an annual basis.

There was no one variable that appeared to be better than the others in identifying value stocks that outperformed the market. In the Lakonishok, Schleifer, and Vishny study, price-to-cash flow was a better indicator of value than price-to-earnings or price-to-book value. In the Calderwood study, value stocks selected on the basis of high dividend yield outperformed those selected on the basis of price-to-book or price-to-earnings by a small margin. In the Bauman, Conover, and Miller study, price-to-book value was a better indicator of value than price-to-earnings, price-to-cash flow, or dividend yield.

The Calderwood study also tested a combination of the three variables. Some stocks were ranked in the top 30% for all three criteria: high dividend yield, low price-to-book value, and low price / earnings. The portfolio of stocks that satisfied all three screening criteria outperformed the portfolios that were ranked on the basis of only one variable.

Table 5-1 Value vs. Growth: A Summary of Empirical Studies

Author	Period of Study	Data Sources	Types of Companies	Variables Tested	Grouped by	Frequency of Rebalancing	Value – Growth Annualized*	Value – Benchmark Annualized
Basu	9/1956–8/1971	Compustat and CRSP	1,400 NYSE-traded industrials	Price-to-earnings	Quintiles	Annual	P/E 6.75%	Vs. sample 4.19%
Lakonishok, Schleifer, and Vishny	1963–1990	Compustat and CRSP	NYSE and AMEX	Price-to-book, price-to-cash flow, price-to-earnings, sales growth rate	Deciles	Annual	P/B 4.5%, P/CF 8.4%, P/E 3.1%, SGR 4.9%	Size adjusted P/B 2.3%, P/CF 3.5%, P/E 1.2%, SGR 2.1%
Fuller, Hulberts, and Levinson	1973–1990	Compustat and Barra	Approx. 1,000 large cap stocks	Price-to-earnings	Quintiles	Annual	P/E 8.0%	Vs. mid quintile 3.1%
Dreman and Berry	1/1973–3/1993	Abel Nosser database, Compustat	995 companies	Price-to-earnings	20%/60%/20%	Annual	P/E 9.8%	Vs. total sample 5.2%
Calderwood	1981–1994	S&P	S&P 500	Dividend yield, price-to-book, price-to-earnings	Top 30%	Quarter		Vs. SP500: DY 5.0%, P/B 4.8%, P/E 4.2, combined 6.8%
Capaul, Rowley, and Sharpe	1/1981–6/1992	S&P, Barra, Union Bank of Switzerland	Indices for France, Germany, Switzerland, UK, Japan, USA	Price-to-book	Two groups	Semiannual	P/B 3.4%	

Harris and Marston	7/1982–12/1989	Compustat, CRSP, IBES	600 companies	Price-to-book, earnings growth rate	30%/40%/30%	Month	P/B 3.2%	
Bauman, Conover, and Miller	1986–1996	Compustat, Global Vantage	21 countries, approx. 2,800 stocks	Price-to-earnings, price-to-cash flow, price-to-ook value, dividend yield	Quartiles	Annual	P/E 4.4%, P/CF 4.3%, P/B 5.7%, DY 4.8%	
Fama and French	7/1963–12/1990	Compustat and CRSP	NYSE, AMEX, NASDAQ	Beta, market cap, price-to-book, price-to-earnings	Deciles	Annual	P/B 11.8%, for small cap 6.9%	Vs. CRSP Index: P/B 4.8%, small cap 2.8%

* Annualized difference between lowest and highest grouping.

Source: Robert G. Kahl, CFA

Higher Returns with Less Risk?

Several of the studies considered risk as measured by beta and standard deviation. Beta is a measure of systematic risk—the tendency of the price of a security to respond to price changes in the broad market. Standard deviation is a measure of dispersion from the mean return of the security. There was little, if any, evidence to support the view that value strategies involve more risk. In fact, Fama and French found evidence to the contrary—stocks with low price-to-book value ratios actually had lower betas.

Earnings Growth—Reversion to the Mean

Attempts to explain the persistent advantage of value stocks over growth stocks focus on reversion to the mean. In pricing a security, investors and analysts naturally take into consideration the expected future growth rates of the company. As future growth rates are difficult to predict, investors and analysts often extrapolate from past growth rates. This process of estimating growth often ignores the tendency of corporate profit growth to revert to the mean.

This phenomenon was clearly demonstrated in a study by Fuller, Huberts, and Levinson. While growth stocks initially experience higher growth rates than value stocks, the higher growth rates do not last long enough to justify the higher price-to-earnings multiples that growth investors have been willing to pay. As Table 5-1 indicates, the stocks were ranked by P/E ratios and divided into quintiles. For the eighteen years ending in March 1991, the lowest P/E quintile outperformed the highest P/E quintile by 8.0% on an annualized, risk-adjusted basis. The quintile with the lowest P/E ratios had a mean ratio of 6.1, while the quintile with the highest P/E ratios had a mean ratio of 44.9.

Fuller et al. analyzed the earnings-per-share (EPS) growth of the different quintiles after each of eight years. After one year, the highest P/E quintile had EPS growth that exceeded the lowest P/E quintile by 18.5%. In years 2 and 3, this EPS growth advantage declined to 7.0% and 3.6%, respectively. For years 4 and 5, the EPS growth advantage was in the 2–3% range. For years 6 through 8, the EPS growth advantage was in the 1–2% range. The earnings growth rates converged close to the mean after only four years. The P/E ratios of the quintiles implied longer periods of high growth for high P/E stocks or low growth for low P/E stocks than what the companies actually experienced.

Earnings growth rates tend to revert to the mean quickly because of the nature of the capital markets. Industries that are experiencing high growth rates tend to attract competition and capital investment by other firms. This competitive process eventually results in lower returns on equity and lower earnings growth rates. Conversely, industries with low growth rates attract less capital investment, and management may attempt to achieve higher earnings by operating more efficiently. Thus, the earnings growth rates of both high and low growth companies tend to revert toward the mean of the economy.

Will the Value Advantage Continue?

Several researchers expect the value investing advantage to continue based upon human behavior. Lakonishok et al. suggest that investors put excessive weight on the recent past in attempting to predict the future. This is a common judgment error in psychological experiments and may explain investor preference for glamour stocks. They also suggest that institutions prefer glamour stocks and are willing to pay a premium for them because they appear to be "prudent" investments. They are easy to justify to sponsors, who erroneously equate high growth companies with good investments.

Investing based upon value factors represents a good default strategy if an investor has a relatively long time horizon. However, as we saw in the last chapter, Research Affiliates recommends that relative valuations be monitored and expectations adjusted accordingly.

Conclusion

For the purpose of establishing investment styles and strategies, value and growth stocks are defined in a variety of ways. Two major data providers, FTSE Russell and Morningstar, use a composite of variables to make the distinction between value and growth stocks.

Nine major studies on value-versus-growth investment strategies were examined. The results of all nine studies were consistent. Value investing strategies outperformed growth strategies. This held true regardless of which variable was used to identify value stocks. Variables that were used to identify value stocks included price-to-earnings, price-to-book value, price-to-cash flow, price-to-free cash flow, and dividend yield. None of the studies found evidence to support the view that value strategies involve more risk.

Although growth stocks initially experience higher growth rates than value stocks, the growth rates of both quickly revert toward the mean. When investing in stocks, investors demonstrate overoptimism for growth stocks and overpessimism for value stocks. Several researchers expect the value investing advantage to continue, although relative valuations should be monitored.

References

Basu, S. "Investment Performance of Common Stocks in Relation to Their Price-Earnings Ratios: A Test of the Efficient Market Hypothesis." *Journal of Finance*, vol. XXXII, no. 3 (June 1977), 663–682. http://www.bellmontsecurities.com.au/wp-content/uploads/2014/10/Investment-Performance-of-Common-Stocks-in-Relation-to-Their-PE-Ratios.pdf

Bauman, W. Scott, C. Mitchell Conover, and Robert E. Miller. "Growth versus Value and Large-Cap versus Small-Cap Stocks in International Markets." *Financial Analysts Journal*, vol. 54, no. 2 (March–April 1998), 75–89. http://www.bengrahaminvesting.ca/research/Papers/Conover/Growth_versus_Value_

and_Large-Cap_versus_Small-Cap_Stocks_in_International_ Markets.pdf

Bender, Jennifer, Remy Briand, Dimitris Melas, and Raman Aylur Subramanian. "Foundations of Factor Investing." *MSCI Research Insight*. December 2013. https://www.msci.com/ resources/pdfs/Foundations_of_Factor_Investing.pdf

Calderwood, Stanford. "The Positive Bias for Value Investors in U.S. Equities," in *Value and Growth Styles in Equity Investing*. Charlottesville, VA: Association for Investment Management and Research, 1995, 4–13. http://www.cfapubs.org/doi/ pdf/10.2469/cp.v1995.n5.2

Capaul, Carlo, Ian Rowley, and William F. Sharpe. "International Value and Growth Stock Returns." *Financial Analysts Journal*, vol. 49, no. 1 (January–February 1993), 27–36. http://www.jstor. org/stable/pdf/4479610.pdf?seq=1#page_scan_tab_contents

Dreman, David N., and Michael A. Berry. "Overreaction, Underreaction, and the Low-P/E Effect." *Financial Analysts Journal*, vol. 51, no. 4 (July–August 1995), 21–30. http://www. cfapubs.org/doi/abs/10.2469/faj.v51.n4.1917

Fama, E. and K. French. "The Cross-section of Expected Stock Returns." *Journal of Finance*, June 1992, 427–465. http://www. bengrahaminvesting.ca/Research/Papers/French/The_Cross-Section_of_Expected_Stock_Returns.pdf

Fuller, Russell J., Lex C. Huberts, and Michael J. Levinson. "Returns to E/P Strategies, Higgledy-Piggledy Growth, Analysts' Forecast Errors, and Omitted Risk Factors." *Journal of Portfolio Management*, vol. 19, no. 2 (Winter 1993), 13–24. https:// www.msci.com/resources/research/articles/barra/ep-strat.pdf

Fuller, Russell J., Lex C. Huberts, and Michael J. Levinson. "It's Not Higgledy-Piggledy Growth!" *Journal of Portfolio Management*, vol. 18, no. 2 (Winter 1992), 38–45. https://www.msci.com/ www/research-paper/it-s-not-higgledy-piggledy/014562213

Hackel, Kenneth S., Joshua Livnat, and Atul Rai. "The Free Cash Flow/Small-Cap Anomaly." *Financial Analysts Journal*, vol. 50, no. 5 (September–October 1994), 33–42. http://www.jstor.org/stable/4479772?seq=1#page_scan_tab_contents

Haugen, Robert A. *The New Finance: The Case against Efficient Markets*. Englewood Cliffs, NJ: Prentice Hall, 1995.

Harris, Robert S., and Felicia C. Marston. "Value versus Growth Stocks: Book-to-Market, Growth, and Beta. *Financial Analysts Journal*, vol. 50, no. 5 (September–October 1994), 18–24. http://www.cfapubs.org/doi/abs/10.2469/faj.v50.n5.18

Lakonishok, J., A. Schleifer, and R. Vishny. "Contrarian Investment, Extrapolation, and Risk." *Journal of Finance*, vol. 49, no. 5 (December 1994), 1541–78. https://www8.gsb.columbia.edu/sites/valueinvesting/files/files/CIER_0.pdf

Nicholson, S. Francis. "Price Ratios in Relation to Investment Results." *Financial Analysts Journal*, vol. 24, no. 1 (January–February 1968), 105–109. http://www.cfapubs.org/doi/abs/10.2469/faj.v24.n1.105?journalCode=faj

CHAPTER 6

Stock Exposure by Market Capitalization

> You don't need to be an expert in order to achieve
> satisfactory investment returns. But if you aren't,
> you must recognize your limitations and follow
> a course certain to work reasonably well. Keep
> things simple and don't swing for the fences.
>
> —Warren Buffett,
> CEO of Berkshire Hathaway

FTSE Russell—US Indices Based on Market Capitalization

Common stocks are often categorized by market capitalization (or cap for short)—large cap, mid cap, and small cap. The delineation between these categories is not always consistent. Some publications refer to the S&P 500 when referring to large cap stocks while others refer to the Russell 1000. The index that is generally referred to when discussing small cap stocks is the Russell 2000.

FTSE Russell has a variety of stock indices and there are many investment products associated with them. FTSE Russell ranks 4,000 US companies on the basis of market capitalization on the last trading day of May each year. The indices are then reconstituted on the basis of the updated rankings. The breakdown of their major indices related to market capitalization follows:

Table 6-1 Major FTSE Russell US Indices Based on Market Capitalization as of May 31, 2015

Index/Subindex	Approximate No. of Stocks	Market Cap Ranking	% of Total US Market Cap	Market Cap ($B)		
				Largest	Average	Median
Russell 3000	3,000	1–3,000	98%	785.5	116.7	1.6
Russell 1000	1,000	1–1,000	92%	785.5	126.3	8.6
Russell Top 200	200	1–200	68%	785.5	176.8	50.4
Russell Midcap	800	201–1,000	28%	37.8	13.8	6.6
Russell 2000	2,000	1001–3,000	8%	11.8	2.2	0.8

Source: www.russell.com/indexes

Morningstar—Market Cap Style Boxes

Morningstar uses a flexible system to categorize the market cap of stocks. Large cap stocks are defined as the group that accounts for 70% of the capitalization of each geographic area. Mid cap stocks represent the next 20%, and small-cap stocks the bottom 10% of capitalization of each geographic area.

The Small Cap Premium

According to Ibbotson SBBI, from 1926 through 2014, small cap stocks returned 12.2% compounded annually, while large cap stocks returned 10.1%. The marginal difference in favor of small cap stocks is often referred to as the small cap premium.

Professors Fama and French have been the biggest proponents of the small cap premium. They proposed a three-factor model to explain equity returns: beta (sensitivity to systemic risk), company size (as measured by market capitalization), and value (based on book-to-market value ratio). Some researchers have questioned the nature of the small cap premium or whether it exists at all.

Assuming the small-cap premium is valid, the explanations that are offered for the better relative performance of small-cap stocks are related to risk. The types of risk associated with small-cap stocks are (1) reduced access to various financing options, (2) lack of market liquidity, and (3) less information available to assess risk.

While small cap stocks have provided higher returns over the entire period from 1926 through 2015, there have been extended periods when large cap stocks have outperformed small cap stocks. Table 6-2 illustrates the alternating performance advantage of small cap and large cap stocks.

Table 6-2 Large Cap versus Small Cap: Periods of Better Relative Performance 1926–2015

Years	No. of Years	Advantage
1926–1932	7	Large
1933–1936	4	Small
1937–1941	5	Large
1942–1945	4	Small
1946–1957	12	Large
1958–1968	11	Small
1969–1973	5	Large
1974–1983	10	Small
1984–1990	7	Large
1991–1994	4	Small
1995–1998	4	Large
1999–2013	15	Small
2014–2015	2	Large

Source: Wisdom Tree and Ibbotson and Associates.

P/E Ratios and Growth Rates

The Leuthold Group tracks the ratio of the small-cap median P/E ratio to S&P 500 P/E ratio. This ratio can vary considerably over time. From 1986 to 2014, the median of the ratio was 0.99. The ratio was as low as 0.6 during much of 2000 and reached a high of 1.38 during 2013. This change in relative valuations accounts for the extended advantage streak of small-cap stocks during the span of 1999 through 2013.

A higher valuation for small-cap stocks may be justified by higher earnings growth. What are the differences in expected earnings growth between large-cap and small-cap stocks? Research Affiliates, a firm that provides research on asset allocation, publishes their real ten-year expected risk and return forecast on their website. As of 2/29/2016, they had the following breakdown of their return assumptions for large and small cap stocks.

Table 6-3 Comparison of Ten-Year Real Expected Returns as of 2/29/2016

Return Components	S&P 500	Russell 2000
Yield	2.1%	1.8%
Growth	1.3%	2.0%
Valuation	–2.0%	–3.0%
Total Real Return	1.4%	0.8%

Source: www.researchaffiliates.com

As the table above indicates, Research Affiliates (RA) expects higher earnings growth from the Russell 2000, offset by a higher dividend yield for the S&P 500. Research Affiliates also expects the valuation levels to decline for both the S&P 500 and the Russell 2000, but to a greater extent for the Russell 2000. While the future is uncertain, the expected returns of Research Affiliates as of 2/29/2016 appear reasonable.

Conclusion

The market capitalization of stocks varies considerably. In the years starting in 1926 to the present, small-capitalization stocks have had a higher compound annual growth rate. Due to a relatively high current valuation level, small-cap stocks are not likely to have superior returns relative to large-cap stocks over the next ten years.

References

"Russell U.S. Equity Indexes—Construction and Methodology." FTSE Russell. December 2015. http://www.ftse.com/products/downloads/Russell-US-indexes.pdf?88

Research Affiliates. "Real 10-Year Expected Risk & Return." http://www.researchaffiliates.com/AssetAllocation/Pages/Core-Overview.aspx

Damodaran, Aswath. "The Small Cap Premium: Where Is the Beef?" Musings on Markets Blog, April 11, 2015. http://aswathdamodaran.blogspot.com/2015/04/the-small-cap-premium-fact-fiction-and.html

Fama, Eugene F. and Kenneth R. French. "The Cross-Section of Expected Stock Returns." *The Journal of Finance*, June 1992. http://www.bengrahaminvesting.ca/Research/Papers/French/The_Cross-Section_of_Expected_Stock_Returns.pdf

Kalesnik, Vitali and Noah Beck. "Busting the Myth about Size." *Research Affiliates—Insights*, November 2014. http://www.researchaffiliates.com/Our%20Ideas/Insights/Fundamentals/Pages/284_Busting_the_Myth_About_Size.aspx

Schwartz, Jeremy. "U.S. Equities: Historical Trends of Large Caps vs. Small Caps." *WisdomTree Blog*, October 22, 2013. http://www.wisdomtree.com/blog/index.php/u-s-equities-historical-trends-of-large-caps-vs-small-caps/

Zimmerman, Trip. "Are You Concerned about Small-Cap Valuations?" *Wisdom Tree Blog.* July 31, 2014. http://www.wisdomtree.com/blog/index.php/are-you-concerned-about-small-cap-valuations/

"Small Caps, Large Opportunity: The Case for Global and International Small-Cap Equity." *Lazard Asset Management Investment Focus*, February 12, 2015. http://www.lazard-net.com/us/docs/sp0/14693/SmallCapsLargeOpportunity_LazardInvestmentFocus.pdf?pagename=Investment+Focus

CHAPTER 7

CAPE Ratios

> Our job is to find a few intelligent things to do, not
> to keep up with every damn thing in the world.
> —Charlie Munger,
> vice chairman of Berkshire Hathaway

Development of the CAPE Ratio

The price-to-earnings ratio is a common metric to assess the reasonableness of a stock's price relative to its earnings. However, the economy and corporate profits are cyclical in nature. Thus, the denominator in the price-to-earnings ratio is not very stable. Benjamin Graham and David Dodd proposed in their book, *Security Analysis*, that a company's earnings power be estimated by taking an average of the past five to ten years.

Robert Shiller and John Campbell used a cyclically adjusted price-to-earnings ratio (CAPE) to estimate dividends and future stock returns of the S&P 500. The denominator of the CAPE ratio that they used in their 1987 study was calculated by taking an average of inflation-adjusted earnings for the prior thirty years. Shiller and Campbell concluded the following:

> Our results indicate that a long moving average of real earnings help to forecast future real dividends. The ratio of this earnings variable to the current stock price is a powerful predictor of the return on stock, particularly when the return is measured over several years. We have shown that these facts make stock prices and (annual) returns much too volatile to accord with a simple present-value model. Yet annual returns do seem to carry some information and are correlated with what they should be given the model.

In other words, the CAPE ratio was not very effective at predicting returns for single years but was effective at predicting average annual returns over longer multiyear periods.

Research regarding the use of the CAPE ratio to predict stock market returns has been extended to other financial markets. Norbert Keimling, Head of Research at StarCapital Research in Germany, examined the relationship between CAPE and subsequent returns of the following fifteen years in fourteen other countries. There was a strong relationship between the CAPE ratio and subsequent returns in all fourteen countries. Lower CAPE ratios resulted in higher subsequent returns, and high CAPE ratios resulted in lower subsequent returns. Attractive CAPE levels of below 8 were followed by high average annual real capital growth of 13.1% over the next fifteen years. In contrast, high CAPE levels above 32 resulted in average annualized capital growth of 0.0% for the subsequent fifteen years.

Valuation-Based Asset Allocation

PortfolioVisualizer.com has a tool to analyze various asset allocation or timing models. One of the allocation models tests the past results of changing the asset allocation between stocks and bonds based upon the Shiller CAPE ratio (price-to-average of ten years of inflation-adjusted earnings). The dynamic asset allocation that was tested was based upon the following rules for asset allocation:

- If CAPE ≥ 22, then 40% stocks and 60% bonds
- If CAPE ≥ 14 but < 22, then 60% stocks and 40% bonds
- If CAPE < 14, then 80% stocks, 20% bonds

PortfolioVisualizer.com is defining stocks as all common stocks incorporated in the US and listed on the NYSE, AMEX, or NASDAQ, excluding ADRs and REITS. Bond returns are based upon the ten-year US Treasury bond.

The table below shows the results of changing the asset allocation based upon the rules above. CAGR is the compound annualized growth rate. Maximum drawdown is the largest decline from peak to trough of the market. The Sharpe ratio is average return in excess of the risk-free rate divided by standard deviation of the portfolio.

The CAPE-based allocation had a higher CAGR than the 60/40 allocation with a lower standard deviation and smaller maximum drawdown. The 100% static allocation in the S&P 500 had the highest CAGR, although many people would find the maximum drawdown to be unacceptable.

Table 7-1 Results of Changing Asset Allocation Based upon Shiller CAPE Ratio January 1988 to December 2015

Portfolio	Final Balance	CAGR	Standard Deviation	Best Year	Worst Year	Maximum Drawdown	Sharpe Ratio
Allocation based on CAPE ratio	$138,846	9.85%	7.97%	31.15%	–3.92%	–18.42%	0.80
60% stocks / 40% bonds	$127,032	9.50%	9.29%	31.15%	–14.87%	–25.98%	0.66
Bond portfolio	$64,125	6.86%	7.12%	22.69%	–7.60%	–11.93%	0.52
S&P 500 total return	$154,678	10.28%	14.48%	37.58%	–37.00%	–50.95%	0.53

Source: PortfolioVisualizer.com

Monitoring Current CAPE Ratios

The CAPE ratio that is most commonly used is an average of inflation-adjusted earnings over a ten-year period. A website that maintains information on the Shiller PE ratio (using a ten-year inflation-adjusted earnings average) and other historical information about the S&P 500 is located at www.multpl.com.

From 1881 through 2015, the median Shiller PE ratio has been 16.0. As of December 2015, the Shiller PE is at 25.8. It has only been this high three times in the past: 1929, 2000, and 2007—all years that were followed by significant market declines.

Research Affiliates, LLC in Newport Beach, California, publishes their real (after inflation) ten-year expected risk and return estimates on their website for all to see. Their estimates for equity returns incorporate a Shiller CAPE ratio. They estimate equity returns for various countries using the following four components:

> equity return = current dividend yield + real earnings growth + change in valuation + currency adjustment

A high Shiller PE ratio will result in a negative value for the change in valuation component as the valuation level would most likely revert toward the mean. Conversely, a low Shiller PE ratio would be expected to result in a positive value for the change in valuation component as the valuation reverts toward the mean. The Research Affiliates estimates can be viewed at http://www.researchaffiliates. com/AssetAllocation/Pages/Core-Overview.aspx.

StarCapital also publishes CAPE ratios and other data for approximately forty countries on their website for public viewing. Their current data can be viewed at http://www.starcapital.de/research/ stockmarketvaluation?SortBy=Shiller_PE.

Conclusion

Use of the CAPE ratio to adjust your equity allocation is a strategy that is likely to reduce the maximum drawdown of a portfolio while maintaining a relatively high return over a longer time horizon of ten years or more.

References

Brightman, Chris. "Investing versus Flipping." Research Affiliates—Fundamentals, October 2015. http://www.researchaffiliates.com/Our%20Ideas/Insights/Fundamentals/Pages/472_Investing_versus_Flipping.aspx

Campbell, John Y. and Robert J. Shiller. "Stock Prices, Earnings, and Expected Dividends." *The Journal of Finance*, vol. 43, no. 3, July 1988. http://scholar.harvard.edu/files/campbell/files/campbellshiller_jf1988.pdf

Faber, Mebane T. "A Quantitative Approach to Tactical Asset Allocation." *The Journal of Wealth Management*, Spring 2007. Updated February 2013. http://papers.ssrn.com/sol3/papers.cfm?abstract_id=962461

Faber, Mebane T. "Everything You Need to Know about the CAPE Ratio." August 22, 2014. http://mebfaber.com/2014/08/22/everything-you-need-to-know-about-the-cape-ratio/

Keimling, Norbert, "CAPE: Predicting Stock Market Returns." StarCapital Research, February 2014. http://www.starcapital.de/docs/2014_02_CAPE_Predicting_Stock_Market_Returns.pdf

CHAPTER 8

Fixed Income Securities

It's the investor's job to intelligently bear risk for profit. Doing it well is what separates the best from the rest.

—Howard Marks,
cofounder of Oaktree Capital Management

Types of Fixed Income Securities

The major types of fixed income securities are the following:

- US Treasury securities are issued by the US Department of Treasury and are backed by the full faith and credit of the US government.
- US agency securities are issued by federal budget agencies or government-sponsored enterprises (GSEs). With the exception of the Tennessee Valley Authority, debt issued by federal budget agencies is backed by the full faith and credit of the US government and is exempt from SEC registration. Debt issued by government-sponsored enterprises is not backed by the full faith and credit of the US government.
- Sovereign debt, as the term is commonly used, is debt issued by countries other than the United States. Sovereign

debt may be issued in local currency terms or in another currency, such as the US dollar or the euro.

- Corporate debt is issued by corporations for a variety of purposes. Corporate debt that is issued with a maturity less than one year is referred to as commercial paper.

- Municipal securities are issued by state and local governments and their creations such as special districts. Generally, interest from these types of securities is tax-exempt. Interest may or may not be taxable at the state and local level. Some municipal issues such as Build America Bonds are taxable at all levels.

- Mortgage pass-through securities are a type of mortgage-backed securities (MBS) that are secured by a collection of residential or commercial mortgages. The cash flow from a mortgage pass-through security will depend on the cash flow of the underlying mortgages and will consist of scheduled principal, interest, and prepayments. Most mortgage pass-through securities are issued by Government National Mortgage Association (GNMA), Federal National Mortgage Association (Fannie Mae), or Federal Home Loan Mortgage Corporation (Freddie Mac) and are referred to as Agency MBS. GNMA is a wholly-owned US government corporation, while Fannie Mae and Freddie Mac are government-sponsored enterprises. As of October 2015, both Fannie Mae and Freddie Mac are under conservatorship with the Federal Housing Finance Agency acting as conservator.

- Collateralized mortgage obligations (CMO) are another type of MBS that are backed by a pool of pass-through securities or a pool of mortgage loans. CMOs are structured so there are several classes of securities (called tranches) with varying maturities. The principal and interest distributions among the tranches are specified by the prospectus.

- Asset-backed securities (ABS) are securities backed by financial assets that are not mortgage loans. They may have either a pass-through structure or they may have different tranches with different characteristics. ABS may be backed by automobile loans, credit card receivables, home equity loans, senior bank loans, SBA loans, or other receivables.

- Preferred stock is a class of shares that has a fixed dividend payment that must be paid before any dividends are paid to common shareholders. Preferred shares have no maturity date but are callable at the option of the corporation. They are subordinate to debt issued by a company but have a superior position to common shares in the event of corporate liquidation. Preferred shares may have features that allow convertibility to common stock.

Credit Ratings

There are three major credit rating agencies in the United States: Standard & Poor's, Moody's Investors Service, and Fitch Ratings. Table 8-1 shows the credit rating symbol classifications of both Standard & Poor's and Moody's Investors Service.

Table 8-1 Credit Rating Symbols

Standard & Poor's			Moody's	
Investment Grade				
AAA	Extremely strong capacity to meet financial commitments. Highest rating.		Aaa	Obligations rated Aaa are judged to be of the highest quality, subject to the lowest level of credit risk.
AA	Very strong capacity to meet financial commitments.		Aa	Obligations rated Aa are judged to be of high quality and are subject to very low level of credit risk.
A	Strong capacity to meet financial commitments, but somewhat susceptible to adverse economic conditions and changes in circumstances.		A	Obligations rated A are judged to be upper-medium grade and are subject to low credit risk.

BBB	Adequate capacity to meet financial commitments, but more subject to adverse economic conditions.	Baa	Obligations rated Baa are judged to be medium-grade and subject to moderate credit risk and, as such, may possess certain speculative characteristics.
Speculative Grade			
BB	Less vulnerable in the near-term but faces major ongoing uncertainties to adverse business, financial, and economic conditions.	Ba	Obligations rated Ba are judged to be speculative and are subject to substantial credit risk.
B	More vulnerable to adverse business, financial and economic conditions but currently has the capacity to meet financial commitments.	B	Obligations rated B are considered speculative and are subject to high credit risk.
CCC	Currently vulnerable and dependent on favorable business, financial and economic conditions to meet financial commitments.	Caa	Obligations rated Caa are judged to be speculative, of poor standing, and are subject to very high credit risk.
CC	Currently highly vulnerable.	Ca	Obligations rated Ca are highly speculative and likely in, or very near, default, with some prospect of recovery of principal and interest.
C	A bankruptcy petition has been filed or similar action taken, but payments of financial commitments are continued.	C	Obligations rated C are the lowest rated and are typically in default, with little prospect for recovery of principal and interest.
D	Payment default on financial commitments.		

Source: Standard & Poor's   Source: Moody's Investors Service

Moody's Investors Service published its 2015 issue of "Corporate Default and Recovery Rates." Below is a graph showing cumulative default rates over twenty years by initial rating category for 3,694 global bonds and loans issued in 1996. As Figure 8-1 demonstrates, cumulative default rates are much higher for the speculative credit ratings.

Figure 8-1 Moody's Cumulative Default Rates by Credit Rating

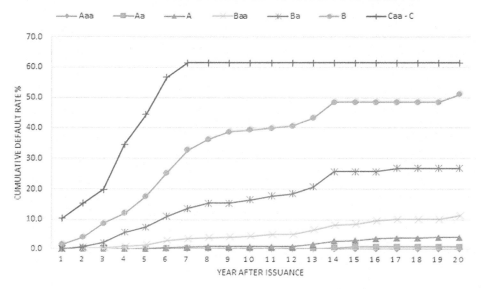

Source of data: Moody's Investors Service

Some credit rating agencies incorporate the potential for recovery into their rating opinions. An estimate of recovery is made that reflects the percentage of outstanding principal that is likely to be recovered in the event of default. Estimated recovery rates may result in positive or negative adjustments to the credit rating of an issue.

Credit Spreads

Credit spreads refer to the additional yield that an investor can achieve relative to a US Treasury security or other benchmark security with a similar maturity or duration. Credit spreads may vary significantly over time.

In the chart below, the B of A Merrill Lynch US Corporate Master Option-Adjusted Spread reflects the spread for US dollar–denominated investment grade (AAA to BBB–) corporate debt, including mortgage and asset-backed securities, which are publicly traded in the domestic market. During the last eight years, the credit spread on this group of bonds was as low as 0.54% in September 1997 and as high as 6.41% in November 2008.

Figure 8-2 US Corporate Bond Spreads—Investment Grade

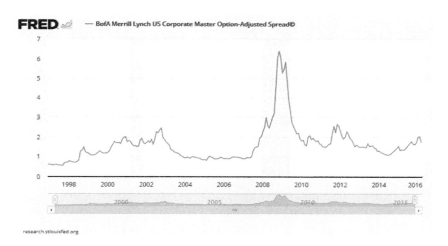

FRED — BofA Merrill Lynch US Corporate Master Option-Adjusted Spread©

research.stlouisfed.org

In the chart below, the B of A Merrill Lynch US High Yield Master II Option-Adjusted Spread reflects the spread for US dollar–denominated corporate debt below investment grade (BB+ and below) that is publicly traded in the US domestic market. During the last eight years, we see that this yield spread was as low as 2.5% in May 2007 and as high as 19.88% in November 2008.

Figure 8-3 US Corporate Bond Spreads—Speculative Grade

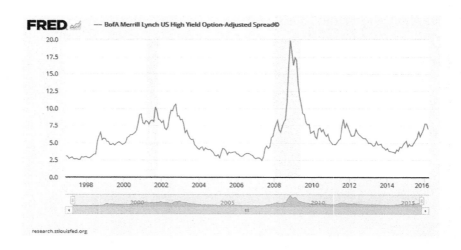

Impact of Changes in Interest Rates

The US Treasury yield curve as of 3/28/2016 is shown below.

Figure 8-4 US Treasury Yield Curve 3/28/2016

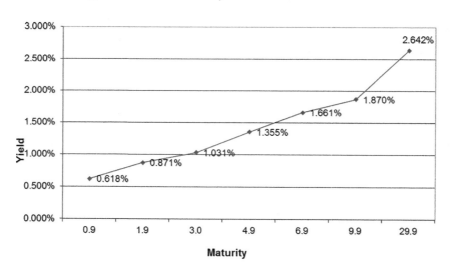

Source: WSJ.com and Robert G. Kahl, CFA

Figure 8-5 shows the impact of changes in interest rates over a one-year period on the total return of US Treasury securities. Total return is equal to the sum of interest income received and the change in the market value of the bond. The light-blue line represents a shift downward in interest rates of 1% for the various maturities with a 0% interest rate floor. The yellow line represents no change in the level of interest rates. The pink and dark-blue lines represent the total return after parallel shifts (the interest rate change is a constant amount across the yield curve) in rates of +1.0% and +2.0%, respectively. Given the low level of interest rates at this time, investors should consider the short/intermediate maturity range unless a high probability is assigned to lower interest rates.

An expansion of credit spreads can also have a negative impact on the total return of lower quality bonds.

Figure 8-5 US Treasuries—Total Returns
One Year After 3/28/2016

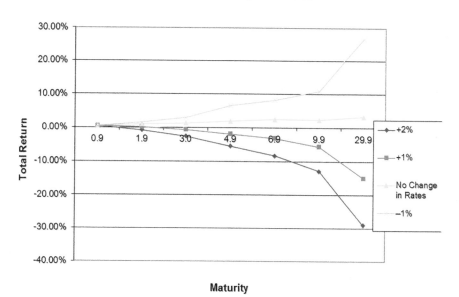

Source: Robert G. Kahl, CFA

Conclusion

For the fixed-income portion of most investors' portfolios, only investment grade securities should be purchased. Credit spreads may increase substantially during recessionary periods or times of financial stress. When credit spreads are high and investors are adequately compensated for the probability of default and potential recovery, it may be appropriate to allocate a portion of an investor's portfolio to some fixed-income securities with lower credit ratings.

In addition to credit quality, investors should also monitor the duration of their fixed-income portfolio for sensitivity to changes in interest rates.

References

Fabozzi, Frank J. and T. Dessa Fabozzi. *Handbook of Fixed Income Securities, Fourth Edition.* Irwin Professional Publishing, 1994.

Federal Reserve Bank of St. Louis—Economic Research. https://research.stlouisfed.org/

Homer, Sidney and Martin L. Leibowitz. *Inside the Yield Book: New Tools for Bond Market Strategy.* Prentice-Hall, Inc., 1972.

Moody's Investors Service. "Rating Symbols and Definitions." February 2016. https://www.moodys.com/sites/products/About MoodysRatingsAttachments/MoodysRatingSymbols andDefinitions.pdf

Moody's Investors Service. "Corporate Default and Recovery Rates, 1920–2015." February 29, 2016. https://www.moodys.com/researchandratings/research-type/default-ratings-analytics/default-studies/003009000/4294965103/4294966848/0/0/-/0/-/-/-/-1/-/-/-/en/global/pdf/-/rra

Securities Industry and Financial Markets Association, Investing in Bond website. http://www.investinginbonds.com/

Standard & Poor's Ratings Services. "Guide to Credit Rating Essentials." http://www.spratings.com/documents/20184/760

102/SPRS_Understanding-Ratings_GRE.pdf/298e606f-ce5b-4ece-9076-66810cd9b6aa

Standard & Poor's Ratings Services. "Ratings Direct - 2014 Annual Global Corporate Default Study and Rating Transitions." April 30, 2015. http://www.nact.org/resources/2014_SP_Global_Corporate_Default_Study.pdf

Wikipedia. https://en.wikipedia.org/wiki/Main_Page

CHAPTER 9

Currencies

Unlike the paper dollar, a dollar defined in law as a weight unit of gold is the monetary standard which simultaneously provides all the primary functions of true standard money: (1) a stable store of value; (2) a stable measure and unit of account; and, (3) a universally accepted means of payment. A gold monetary standard combines, in one monetary article of wealth, the three primary functions of money.

—Lewis E. Lehrman,
author of *The True Gold Standard*

Evolution of the International Monetary System

The first coin is believed to be the Lydian trite, minted around 600 BC in Lydia, Asia Minor (in Turkey today). It was made of electrum, an alloy of gold and silver. During the next few centuries, the use of coins quickly spread to Greece and other parts of the world.

During the Middle Ages, the Byzantine gold solidus (or bezant) was used widely throughout Europe and the Mediterranean. As the Byzantine Empire declined, the use of silver coins became more popular in Europe.

In the modern era, Britain established a gold specie standard in 1821 after introducing the gold sovereign coin. Other countries followed with their own gold specie standard: Canada (1853), Newfoundland (1865), the United States and Germany (1873). Australia, New Zealand, and the British West Indies adopted the British gold standard. In the late nineteenth century, some countries such as Mexico, Philippines, and India were on a silver standard, but they pegged their currencies to Britain or the US, which were on a gold standard. By 1908, only China and Hong Kong remained on a silver standard.

During World War I, Britain, Germany, and several other countries involved in the conflict effectively abandoned their gold standards. Government budget and balance of payments deficits would have quickly depleted their gold reserves. Government debt was used to finance the war, which led to higher inflation.

In 1925, the British Gold Standard Act introduced the gold bullion standard and repealed the gold specie standard, ending the circulation of gold coins in Britain. The law allowed the public to convert Bank of England notes into gold bullion—if the minimum size of 400 ounces could be met. The conversion rate for currency notes to gold was established at prewar levels, even though the price level had nearly doubled since then. The conversion of British pound notes into gold accelerated in 1931, leading to a suspension of conversion of currency notes into gold. The Gold Standard Amendments Act of 1931 was passed, and Britain and its trading partners have never returned to a domestic gold standard, where notes issued by the central bank could be converted to gold by the general public.

In the United States, the Gold Reserve Act (January 1934) required all gold and gold certificates held by the Federal Reserve to be surrendered and vested in the title of the US Department of the Treasury. The law banned private possession of gold or the export of gold and forced individuals to sell their gold to the US Treasury. It also changed the nominal price of gold from $20.67 per troy ounce to $35. The revaluation of gold resulted in the increased importation of gold into the United States. US Treasury holdings of gold increased from 6,358 metric tonnes in 1930 to 19,543 metric tonnes by 1940.

On July 22, 1944, the Bretton Woods agreement was signed by forty-four Allied nations in Bretton Woods, New Hampshire. The agreement called for a pegged currency system in which nations were to maintain exchange rates within a ±1% band to the US dollar, which served as the reserve currency. To bolster confidence in the US dollar as reserve currency, the United States agreed to link the US dollar to gold at a rate of $35 per ounce of gold. At this rate, foreign governments and central banks were able to exchange US dollars for gold. Thus, US dollars were considered "as good as gold."

During the 1960s, the market price of gold was often higher than the official fixed rate of $35 per ounce. In November 1961, the London Gold Pool was established to maintain the fixed exchange rate system and maintain the $35 per ounce price in the London gold market. The supporting members of the London Gold Pool were the United States and seven European countries who would sell some of their gold to maintain the $35 price. By 1968, the member nations were no longer willing to continue selling their gold, and the London Gold Pool was abandoned. Central banks began converting more of their US dollars to gold, especially France.

In August 1971, President Nixon signed an executive order to prevent the further conversion of US dollars to gold. At the time, US gold reserves had declined to 8,584 metric tonnes from a maximum of 20,663 metric tonnes in 1952.

One contributing factor in the US dollar's dominance in the international monetary system after 1971 was the agreement negotiated by President Nixon and Secretary of State Henry Kissinger with Saudi Arabia in 1971. Saudi Arabia agreed to denominate all future oil sales in US dollars in exchange for arms and protection from the US. Other OPEC countries agreed to similar deals and the "petro-dollar" was born. The requirement to pay for OPEC oil with US dollars created additional demand by other central banks for US dollars. Thus, the US dollar kept its status as the primary reserve currency in the international monetary system even though the link to gold was no longer in place.

Balance of Payments and Currency Reserves

Countries measure their transactions with the rest of the world using two types of accounts: the current account and the capital account. The current account records trade in goods and services plus transfer payments. Transfer payments consist of remittances, gifts, and grants. The capital account records purchases and sales of assets such as stocks, bonds, land, and other financial assets. The balance of payments is the sum of transactions in both the current and capital accounts.

Foreign currency reserves that central banks hold consist of gold and currency, deposits, or financial securities denominated in the major currencies. The United States dollar and euro are the two dominant reserve currencies, but the UK pound, Japanese yen, Canadian dollar, and Australian dollar are also used. The Chinese renminbi is also being used increasingly for international trade settlement and is in the process of establishing itself as a reserve currency.

When a country has a balance of payments deficit, it must use its currency reserves to cover the deficit. Conversely, if a country has a balance of payments surplus, it will accumulate more foreign currency reserves.

Purchasing Power Parity

The purchasing power parity theorem posits that identical goods will have the same price in different markets absent transaction costs and/or trade barriers when prices are expressed in the same currency. In order to move toward an equilibrium state where trade flows are balanced among countries, currency exchange rates should have a tendency to move toward a rate representing purchasing power parity among countries. Otherwise, the balance of trade remains unbalanced. However, currency markets can trade in a manner inconsistent with the purchasing power parity theorem for an extended period of time for a variety of reasons.

Table 9-1 shows the computation of purchasing power parity (PPP) estimates for several currencies, ranked by the most expensive to the least expensive currency. The ratio of 2014 GDP per capita in US dollars to per capita GDP in PPP terms equals the PPP estimate at the end of 2014. In the next three columns, we calculate the change in the currency since the end of December 2014. Since few countries have yet reported GDP per capita for 2015, we can use the change in exchange rates during 2015 to estimate PPP at the end of 2015. The final column on the right is the product of the 2014 PPP estimate multiplied by the ratio of ending/beginning 2015 exchange rates, which yields the PPP at the end of 2015.

If the PPP estimate in the right-hand column is above a ratio of 1, the currency buys more in the US than the home country. The PPP ratio is below 1 if a currency buys less in the US than the home country. If we look at China, for an example, GDP per capita as of December 2014 is US$ 3,866 based on nominal exchange rates. Using purchasing power parity estimates to estimate the equivalent amount of goods and services that a US worker could buy, China's GDP per capita is US$ 12,609. The third numerical column from the left shows the ratio of nominal GDP to PPP-adjusted GDP per capita. For China, the ratio is 0.307 at the end of December 2014. The value of goods and services produced by China is considerably higher if we assign the same prices to equivalent goods and services that are produced in the United States.

Table 9-1 Purchasing Power Parity Estimates

	2014 GDP per Capita			Exchange Rates			
Country	USD	USD PPP	PPP Estimate 12/31/2014	12/31/2014	12/31/2015	Ratio	PPP Estimate 12/31/2015
Switzerland	58,997	54,983	1.073	1.0097	1.0073	0.998	1.070
Japan	37,595	35,635	1.055	0.0084	0.0083	0.988	1.042
United Kingdom	40,968	37,614	1.089	1.5573	1.4802	0.950	1.035
Euro area	32,789	36,925	0.888	1.2142	1.0906	0.898	0.798
Australia	37,828	43,219	0.875	0.8185	0.7298	0.892	0.780
Canada	38,293	42,817	0.894	0.8620	0.7209	0.836	0.748
Mexico	8,626	16,496	0.523	0.0678	0.0576	0.850	0.444
China	3,866	12,609	0.307	0.1624	0.1540	0.948	0.291
Brazil	5,970	15,412	0.387	0.3758	0.2523	0.671	0.260
Russia	6,844	23,293	0.294	0.0169	0.0136	0.805	0.236

Sources: TradingEconomics.com and Oanda.com

Table 9-1 illustrates that currencies were undervalued relative to the US dollar at the end of December 2014 (where the PPP estimate is below 1) became even more undervalued during 2015. The two most expensive currencies at the end of 2014 (Switzerland and Japan) were among the strongest foreign currencies in 2015. Based upon the purchasing power parity estimates at the end of 2015, an American tourist that goes to Brazil or Russia and exchanges US dollars for the local currency should be able to nearly quadruple their purchasing power.

Dynamics of Currency Volatility in Emerging Economies

In his book *The Volatility Machine*, Michael Pettis analyzes the process that has led to financial market disruptions in many emerging economies. He argues that the degree of a financial crisis is largely a factor of capital structure vulnerability. The capital structure of a country (both sovereign and private debt) can be arranged in such a way that external shocks mechanically lead to "incoherent states." He writes:

> When the structure is lined up in this way, the country has stepped into what I call a "capital structure trap," or a funding strategy that does two things: 1) It links financial or debt servicing costs to the economy in an *inverted* way. 2) More dramatically, it locks the borrower and its creditors into self-reinforcing behavior in which small changes, good or bad, can force players to behave in ways that exacerbate the changes... The capital structure trap consists of an *inverted* liability structure in which an external shock can force both the borrower's revenue and its debt servicing expense to move sharply in an adverse direction.

The types of policies or circumstances that exacerbate negative currency volatility include the following:

- Foreign governments and corporations often borrow in US dollars rather than their local currency. If the local currency experiences a decline, the US dollar debt becomes more difficult to service.

- In recent years, many Eastern European consumers used mortgages denominated in Swiss francs to finance their homes. The lower interest rate appeared enticing, but the loans became much more difficult to service when the Swiss franc appreciated against their local currencies.

- Some countries may depend heavily on one or two commodities (such as oil or iron ore) that experience price volatility. A decline in the price of those commodities will have a negative impact on their export revenue and balance of payments.

- A country may depend on imported goods that are priced in a foreign currency. A decline in the local currency will result in higher prices for imported goods.

- Reliance on foreign capital flows may impact the currency rate. Also, the nature of foreign capital investment will have an impact. Are foreign investors buying real estate or investing in businesses that are illiquid and relatively long term? Or are they buying securities that can be sold at a moment's notice when the economy faces adverse conditions?

Impact of Currency Devaluation on Financial Markets

Currency devaluations are often accompanied by higher interest rates as capital starts to leave the country. The disruptive nature of a currency devaluation often has a negative impact on the economy as it is more difficult to conduct business. Investors may move money from banks and fixed-income securities to common stocks because they represent a superior inflation hedge. However, investors in common stocks of countries that experience currency devaluations generally lose purchasing power compared to investors that have money in a stable currency.

Table 9-2 illustrates the point with a sampling of countries that experienced currency devaluations. The extent of the currency devaluations varies. Three of the countries had declines in the stock market price index during the period of devaluation while the other five had positive returns in their stock markets in local currency terms. However, only one country's stock market (Japan) had a positive return when measured in US dollars.

Table 9-2 Selected Currency Devaluations
and Related Stock Markets

Country	Period	Duration (Months)	Currency	Index	Currency % Change vs. US$	Index % Change in Local Currency	Total Gain/ Loss (in US$)
Sweden	8/15/1992– 3/15/1993	7.0	Krona	OMX Stockholm 30 Index	–31.7%	26.7%	**–13.4%**
United Kingdom	8/15/1992– 2/15/1993	6.0	Pound	London FTSE 100	–22.0%	20.8%	**–5.8%**
Mexico	10/15/1994– 9/2/1998	46.6	Peso	Mexico IPC	–66.5%	14.5%	**–61.6%**
Indonesia	7/1/1997– 7/7/1998	12.2	Rupiah	Jakarta Composite Index	–83.7%	–35.4%	**–89.4%**
Russia	1/13/1998– 8/31/1998	7.6	Ruble	Moscow RTS Index	–59.5%	–80.8%	**–92.2%**
Brazil	1/12/1999– 3/3/1999	1.7	Real	Brazil IBOVESPA	–44.2%	54.7%	**–13.7%**
Argentina	1/3/2002– 6/26/2002	5.8	Peso	Merval Index	–74.0%	–2.5%	**–74.7%**
Japan	9/27/2012– 6/29/2015	33.1	Yen	Nikkei 225	–37.1%	126.1%	**42.2%**

Source: Yahoo Finance and Oanda.com

Can a Reserve Currency Be Devalued?

The last year in which the US current account had a surplus was 1991. Since then, the US has experienced a steady decline in its current account to the low point of the third quarter of 2006 when it hit a quarterly deficit of $216.1 billion. As of the fourth quarter of 2015, the US current account deficit on a quarterly basis stood at $125.3 billion.

Figure 9-1 US Current Account—Quarterly in US$ millions

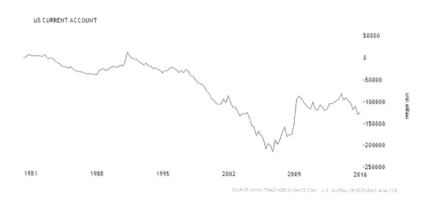

For most countries, a persistent current account deficit of this magnitude would lead to a currency devaluation. The United States, however, has provided the most widely used reserve currency for the world. Trading partners have been willing to accumulate US dollar reserves as a result of their trade surpluses with the United States. Since the US dollar has often been used for trade settlement between countries other than the US, dollar reserves are accumulated from these transactions as well. As a result, current account deficits by the US are allowed to continue, and the net international investment position (difference between a country's external financial assets and liabilities) of the United States has continued to deteriorate to a negative $7.27 trillion at the end of the third calendar quarter of 2015.

Figure 9-2 US Net International Investment Position—Cumulative in US$ millions

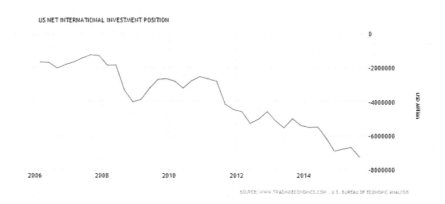

In the past, the natural foreign buyers of US Treasury debt were oil-exporting countries, Japan and China. These countries accumulated US Treasury debt as a result of their trade surpluses with the US and other countries that paid them with US dollars. China has kept their holdings of US Treasury securities at a constant level since the end of 2013, although they have continued to have large trade surpluses. Japan ceased to have consistent trade surpluses in 2011. Oil-exporting countries have seen their trade balances deteriorate since the price of oil began to decline in the summer of 2014. The natural buyers of US Treasury securities in the past are no longer consistent buyers.

The data in Table 9-3 is from the Treasury International Capital System (TIC) and shows the major foreign holders by country of US Treasury securities as of September 2015. China and Japan are the largest holders of US Treasury securities. These two countries alone account for 39.9% of the major foreign holdings.

Table 9-3 Major Foreign Holdings of US
Treasury Securities—September 2015

Country	US$ billions
China, Mainland	1,258
Japan	1,177
Caribbean Banking Centers	323
Oil Exporters	291
Brazil	252
Ireland	223
Switzerland	228
United Kingdom	214
Hong Kong	199
Luxembourg	191
Taiwan	178
Belgium	136
India	114
Singapore	123
Russia	89
Germany	83
All other	1,024
Total	6,103

Source: US Treasury International Capital System

Table 9-4 summarizes TIC data and shows the net purchases of US long-term securities (US Treasury bonds, agency bonds, corporate bonds, and corporate stocks) during the third calendar quarter of 2015. The table is ranked by largest purchasers to largest sellers. The two largest holders of US Treasury securities were the largest net sellers of US securities for the quarter. The three largest net buyers are the Cayman Islands, UK, and France. It is difficult to determine to what extent they are serving as agents for entities in other countries. These capital flows often change substantially from one month to the next, but there no longer appear to be natural and consistent foreign buyers of US securities.

Table 9-4 Foreign Net Purchases of US Long-Term Securities—July–September 2015

Country	US$ millions
Cayman Islands	29,846
United Kingdom	28,721
France	13,926
Taiwan	13,854
Canada	10,845
Germany	5,343
Norway	4,363
Singapore	(3,899)
Brazil	(4,475)
Belgium	(4,592)
Poland	(5,332)
India	(6,770)
Hong Kong	(8,438)
Luxembourg	(10,116)
Mexico	(10,589)
Japan	(11,699)
China, Mainland	(48,786)
All other countries	(590)
Subtotal	(8,388)
ABS repayments and stock swaps	(42,885)
Adjusted total	(51,273)

Source: US Treasury International Capital System

In the absence of continued significant foreign demand for US investments, the US dollar will have to decline in value relative to other currencies in order to spur exports and reduce the trade deficit.

What Next?

In October 2013, both the International Monetary Fund (IMF) and the World Bank held their annual meetings in Washington, DC. At the meetings, Christine Lagarde, IMF managing director, and Jim Kim, World Bank president, expressed their concerns about the potential for a US debt default as the US Congress was debating an increase in the debt ceiling authorization. Earlier in the same week, Mr. Zhu Guangyao, China's vice finance minister, called on US politicians to "ensure the safety of the Chinese investments." At the time, the Chinese government and its citizens held about $1.3 trillion in US Treasury debt, so they had reason to be concerned. Aside from the issue of credit quality of US Treasury debt, which supports the use of the US dollar as a reserve currency, there appears to be a shared desire by many countries to be more independent of US influence.

The G20 (Group of Twenty) countries announced in September 2009 that it would replace the G8 as the main economic council of major nations. The G20 consists of a mix of the world's largest advanced and emerging economies, representing about two-thirds of the world's population, 85% of global GDP and over 75% of global trade. The members of the G20 are Argentina, Australia, Brazil, Canada, China, France, Germany, India, Indonesia, Italy, Japan, South Korea, Mexico, Russia, Saudi Arabia, South Africa, Turkey, United Kingdom, United States, and the European Union. Summit meetings for national leaders are now held on an annual basis, with numerous meetings held throughout the year for staff members to make progress on a variety of issues.

The G20 Agenda proposed by Russia for the September 2013 Summit in Saint Petersburg listed international financial architecture reform as one of the main priorities, including "issues of global liquidity, capital flows, reserve currencies, exchange rates, etc." While it appears that these issues are no longer a high priority for the G20, other international organizations have taken the baton.

There are ongoing efforts to develop alternatives to the IMF and World Bank and to be more independent of US economic leadership. In July 2014, an agreement was signed at the BRICS (Brazil, Russia, India, China, and South Africa) summit meeting to establish the New Development Bank with US$100 billion of total capital to be paid in over seven years.

In addition to the BRICS Development Bank, the BRICS Contingency Fund was established to promote international financial stability by providing "temporary resources to BRICS members facing pressure in their balance of payments." The BRICS Contingency Fund is to have $100 billion in capital and is expected to be operational by the end of August 2015.

In June 2015, delegates from fifty-seven countries attended a signing ceremony in Beijing for the creation of another development bank—the Asian Infrastructure Investment Bank (AIIB). The AIIB will initially be funded with US$50 billion, but it is due to rise to $100 billion. In an embarrassing turnabout, several US allies—including Australia, Germany, the UK, and South Korea—signed the agreement after the US announced that it would not be joining the AIIB.

The Shanghai Cooperation Organization (SCO) is a Eurasian organization that seeks political, economic, and military cooperation. The current member countries are China, Russia, Kazakhstan, Kyrgyzstan, Tajikistan, and Uzbekistan. India and Pakistan have been approved and are expected to join in 2016. Observer states that may join in the future are Afghanistan, Belarus, Iran, and Mongolia. One of long-term objectives of the SCO is to establish a free-trade area among member countries. At the 2008 summit meeting, Russian Prime Minister Vladimir Putin made the following statement: "We now clearly see the defectiveness of the monopoly in world finance and the policy of economic selfishness. To solve the current problem Russia will take part in changing the global financial structure so that it will be able to guarantee stability and prosperity in the world and to ensure progress."

Meanwhile, China is increasing the international use of its currency through currency swaps, settlement of international trade transactions in RMB / yuan, and investment facilities. As of May 2015, there were thirty-one countries that had established currency swap agreements with China, totaling RMB 3.14 trillion (US$ 492 billion), although most of the swaps have yet to be drawn on. Another obstacle to wider of use of the RMB currency is that China remains reluctant to completely open its capital markets to foreigners.

Jim Rickards, author of *Currency Wars*, believes that the international monetary system will ultimately abandon the US dollar as the reserve currency and revert to gold-based settlement:

> The path of the dollar is unsustainable and therefore the dollar will not be sustained.... The SDR solution is being promoted by some global elites in the G20 finance ministries and IMF executive suites, yet to the extent that it simply replaces national paper currencies with a global paper currency, it risks its own rejection and instability in time. A studied, expertly implemented return to the gold standard offers the best chance of stability but commands so little academic respect as to be a nonstarter in current debates. This leaves chaos as a strong possibility. Within chaos, however, there is a second chance to go for gold, albeit in a sudden, unstudied way.

Conclusion

The US dollar was a relatively strong currency in 2015, but it was relatively expensive based upon purchasing power parity estimates at the end of the year. Investors should consider the potential currency risk of their investments as currency devaluations generally have a negative impact on the financial markets associated with them. Given the trend of capital flows and international developments, the continuation of the US dollar's reserve currency status is questionable. Although US investors naturally have a US currency bias, there are diversification benefits from the inclusion of securities that are denominated in foreign currencies in an investment portfolio.

References

Green, Timothy. "Central Bank Gold Reserves: A Historical Perspective since 1845." World Gold Council, Research Study No. 23. November 1999. http://www.newworldeconomics.com/archives/2014/081714_files/WGC%20central%20bank%20gold%20reserves.pdf

Hamilton, Chris. "The Fed's Backdoor QE—Central Bank Currency Swaps?" May 11, 2015. http://econimica.blogspot.com/2015/05/the-feds-backdoor-qe-central-bank.html

Hamilton, Chris. "Veneer of US Growth & Normalcy Has Worn Paper Thin… Reality Plainly Visible Through the Fraud." May 8, 2015. http://econimica.blogspot.com/2015/05/veneer-of-us-growth-normalcy-has-worn.html

Hewitt, Duncan. "Fifty Countries Sign Up to China-Led Asian Infrastructure Investment Bank, in Diplomatic Victory for Beijing." International Business Times, June 29, 2015. http://www.ibtimes.com/fifty-countries-sign-china-led-asian-infra-structure-investment-bank-diplomatic-1987459

Mandrasescu, Valentin. "BRICS Morphing into Anti-Dollar Alliance." SputnikNews.com, July 3, 2014. http://sputniknews.com/voiceofrussia/2014_07_03/BRICS-is-morphing-into-an-anti-dollar-alliance-6229/

Pettis, Michael. *The Volatility Machine: Emerging Economies and the Threat of Financial Collapse.* Oxford University Press, 2001.

Rickards, James. *Currency Wars: The Making of the Next Global Crisis.* Penguin Group, 2011.

Zhu, Yihong. "Swap Agreements & China's RMB Currency Network." Center for Strategic & International Studies (CogitAsia)—a blog of the CSIS Asia Program. May 22, 2015. http://cogitasia. com/swap-agreements-chinas-rmb-currency-network/

"Gold Standard Act of 1925 (England)." Encyclopedia of Money. http://encyclopedia-of-money.blogspot.com/2010/03/gold-standard-act-of-1925-england.html

"The Collapse of the Petrodollar: Oil Exporters Are Dumping US Assets at a Record Pace." April 15, 2015. http://www.zero-hedge.com/news/2015-04-15/collapse-petrodollar-oil-export-ers-are-dumping-us-assets-record-pace

"$100bn BRICS monetary fund to be operational in 30 days." The BRICS Post, July 1, 2015. http://thebricspost.com/100bn-brics-monetary-fund-to-be-operational-in-30-days/#.VdvLdOeFPcs

"The Russian Presidency of the G20: Outline." December, 2012. http://en.g20russia.ru/docs/g20_russia/outline

"Turkish G20 Presidency Priorities for 2015." December, 2014. https://g20.org/wp-content/uploads/2014/12/2015-TURKEY-G-20-PRESIDENCY-FINAL.pdf

US Department of the Treasury International Capital System. https://www.treasury.gov/resource-center/data-chart-center/tic/Pages/index.aspx

www.tradingeconomics.com

https://en.wikipedia.org/wiki/Bretton_Woods_system

https://en.wikipedia.org/wiki/Gold_standard

https://en.wikipedia.org/wiki/Gold_Reserve_Act

https://en.wikipedia.org/wiki/Reserve_currency

https://en.wikipedia.org/wiki/Petrodollar

https://en.wikipedia.org/wiki/Shanghai_Cooperation_Organisation

CHAPTER 10

Precious Metals

Gold is a currency... We have dollars, we have euros, we have yen, and we have gold... The capacity to move money into gold in a large number is extremely limited... If you're going to own a currency, it's not sensible not to own gold... If you don't own gold, there's no sensible reason other than you don't know history and you don't know the economics of it... View it in terms of an alternative form of cash. And also view it as a hedge against what the other parts of your portfolio are—traditional financial assets—in that context, as a diversifier, there should be a piece of that in gold.

> —Ray Dalio, founder of Bridgewater Associates, at the Council on Foreign Relations, September 2012

Gold... has two significant shortcomings, being neither of much use nor procreative. True, gold has some industrial and decorative utility, but the demand for these purposes is both limited and incapable of soaking up new production.

Meanwhile, if you own one ounce of gold for an eternity, you will still own one ounce at its end.
—Warren Buffett, 2011 Berkshire-Hathaway Letter to Shareholders

In the late 1990s renewed buying of physical silver ensued. It began through a large trading firm by a major investor, Warren Buffett's Berkshire Hathaway…which accumulated nearly 130 million ounces from 1997 to early 1998.
—Miguel Perez-Santalla at Bullion Vault, March 2014

There's always a higher risk in fiat currency than there is in gold because gold cannot be created out of thin air like paper currency.
James Turk, founder of GoldMoney Inc.

The Half-Life of Paper Money

In his article "Fate of Paper Money" (June 2008), Mike Hewitt lists 177 currencies that are currently in circulation. The median age for an active currency is thirty-seven years. Of the currencies that are no longer in existence, he writes:

> Excluding the early paper currencies of China up until the 15th century and the majority of paper currencies that existed in China until 1935, there are 609 currencies no longer in circulation. Of these, at least 153 were destroyed as a result of hyperinflation caused by over-issuance. The remainder were revalued, destroyed by military occupation/liberation, renamed for political reasons, or were converted to another currency. The median age for these currencies is only seventeen years.

In the United States, few people question the intrinsic value of paper money. However, the history of paper money should not inspire a sense of complacency.

Gold

Gold is one of the least reactive chemical elements and is one of the most malleable of metals. It has been highly valued for jewelry, coinage, and other purposes for more than five thousand years.

According to the World Gold Council (WGC), at the end of 2014, approximately 183,600 metric tonnes of gold were held in stocks above ground. This is roughly equivalent to a cube twenty-one meters on each side.

Table 10-1 Gold—2014 Global Physical Supply and Demand

	Metric Tonnes	% of Total
Supply		
Mine production	3,133.5	68.3%
Scrap	1,168.9	25.5%
Net ETFs and similar products	184.2	4.0%
Net hedging supply	100.5	2.2%
Total supply	4,587.1	100.0%
Demand		
Jewelry	2,485.3	56.1%
Technology fabrication	346.5	7.8%
Coins and bars	1,004.4	22.7%
Central banks and other institutions	590.5	13.3%
Total physical demand	4,426.7	100.0%
Net surplus/(deficit)	160.4	3.6%

Source: World Gold Council, *Gold Demand Trends* (second Quarter 2015)

The World Gold Council is the source cited most often for gold supply and demand estimates. Its quarterly publication, *Gold Demand Trends* (second quarter 2015), had estimates of gold supply and demand for 2014.

There is some controversy about estimates of global gold demand. The demand estimates from the WGC have been inconsistent with the delivery reports from the Shanghai Gold Exchange (SGE), the world's largest physical gold exchange. The SGE Chairman, Mr. Xu Luode, said at the London Bullion Market Association Forum in Singapore in June 2014:

> Last year, China imported 1,540 tonnes of gold. Such imports, together with the 430 tonnes of gold we produced ourselves, means that we have, in effect, supplied approximately 2,000 tonnes of gold last year. The 2,000 tonnes of gold were consumed by consumers in China... last year, our gold exchange's inventory reduced by nearly 2,200 tonnes, of which 200 tonnes was recycled gold.

Koos Jansen, a precious metals analyst who writes for BullionStar.com in Singapore, has been researching the Chinese gold market extensively, including the Shanghai Gold Exchange. He believes that the WGC is "deliberately understating Chinese physical gold demand to not shock the global gold market." After exchanging e-mails with Thomson Reuters, which provides data for the World Gold Council, he confirmed that the WGC / Thomson Reuters data does not include gold withdrawn directly from the SGE vaults by individual and institutional investors that goes into storage or inventory. The Chinese demand estimate by WGC / Thomson Reuters only includes jewelry and bullion bars / coins sold at the retail level, and all industrial demand. As a result, Jansen believes that WGC's Chinese gold demand estimate may be understated by as much as 1,000 tonnes or more per year.

Another aspect of Chinese gold demand is government ownership of gold. On July 17, 2015, the People's Bank of China (PBOC, China's central bank) announced that their official gold reserves had increased to 1,658 tonnes. This represented an increase of 604 tonnes from its prior disclosure in 2009. Some analysts expected PBOC gold reserves to be much higher and have suggested that China is concealing their government's purchases by using sovereign wealth funds and commercial banks as intermediaries. China has two large sovereign wealth funds that could be used for gold purchases: China Investment Corporation (CIC) and the State Administration of Foreign Exchange Investment Company (SAFE) with estimated capital of $747 and $547 billion, respectively.

Silver

In contrast to gold, most of the silver supply from mines and scrap is used up by industrial fabrication. According to the Silver Institute, global mine production of silver in 2014 amounted to 27,294 metric tonnes (using a conversion factor of 32,150.42 troy ounces per metric tonne).

The Silver Institute has the following estimates for 2014 physical supply and demand:

Table 10-2 Silver—2014 Global Physical Supply and Demand

	M Ounces	Metric Tonnes	% of Total
Supply			
Mine production	877.5	27,293.6	82.6%
Scrap	168.5	5,241.0	15.9%
Net hedging supply	15.8	491.4	1.5%
Total supply	1,061.8	33,026.0	100.0%
Demand			
Jewelry	215.2	6,693.5	20.2%
Coins and bars	196.0	6,096.3	18.4%
Silverware	60.7	1,888.0	5.7%
Industrial fabrication			
Electrical and electronics	263.9	8,208.3	24.7%
Brazing alloys and solders	66.1	2,056.0	6.2%
Photography	45.6	1,418.3	4.3%
Photovoltaic	59.9	1,863.1	5.6%
Other industrial	159.4	4,957.9	14.9%
Subtotal industrial fabrication	594.9	18,503.6	55.8%
Total physical demand	1,066.8	33,181.5	100.0%
Net surplus/deficit	(5.0)	(155.5)	-0.5%

Source: Silver Institute and Thomson Reuters GFMS, World Silver Survey 2015

Price Manipulation

Price manipulation in the precious metals market has been blatant on numerous occasions. Since 2011, there have been large sell orders placed within a few minutes, typically during the most thinly traded periods of the day on the Comex Globex system, which is open twenty-four hours per day. If you have real gold or silver to sell, you certainly wouldn't want to place large orders in this manner to get the best price. Such orders are designed to move the price lower in spite of supply and demand for the physical metals. As Dr. Paul Craig

Roberts, a former assistant secretary of the US Treasury and journalist, explains:

> The price of bullion in the futures market has been falling as demand for physical bullion increases and supply experiences constraints. What we are seeing in the physical market indicates a rising price. Yet in the futures market in which almost all contracts are settled in cash and not with bullion deliveries, the price is falling... it is easy to increase the supply of gold in the futures market where price is established simply by printing uncovered (naked) contracts. Selling naked shorts is a way to artificially increase the supply of bullion in the futures market where price is determined. The supply of paper contracts representing gold increases, but not the supply of physical bullion.

It is unclear exactly who is involved in the price suppression of gold and silver, but it certainly has enabled large quantities of gold and silver bullion to be sold to China and India at modest prices. Ted Butler, a precious metals analyst, believes that the "terminal point" of price manipulation comes when prices get so out of line with physical supply and demand that different entities get attracted to the low price and come into the futures market to buy contracts with the intent of taking delivery.

Comex-registered gold (available for delivery on futures contracts) has declined substantially from 5.2 million ounces in 2006 to 228,761 ounces as of February 5, 2016. The ratio of open interest/registered gold has reached a very high level of 173.8. A normal range for this ratio during the years 2000–2007 was about 10. The normal range moved higher to about 20 during the 2009–2013 period. This ratio now suggests that many sellers of gold contracts on the Comex may not be able to make delivery if requested to do so.

SPDR Gold Trust (GLD)

The SPDR Gold Trust (GLD) is a trust designed to issue shares in exchange for gold bullion and distribute gold bullion in exchange for a minimum basket size of 100,000 shares. Baskets may be created or redeemed only by "authorized participants" who pay a transaction fee for each order to create or redeem baskets of shares. The sponsor is World Gold Trust Services, LLC, a wholly-owned subsidiary of the World Gold Council. The Trustee is Bank of New York Mellon and the custodian of the trust assets is HSBC Bank PLC.

Some of the features of the trust listed in the prospectus dated July 17, 2015 raise concerns about the ability of the trust to perform as expected. Below are some excerpts from the prospectus:

- There is a risk that some or all of the Trust's gold bars held by the Custodian or any subcustodian on behalf of the Trust could be lost, damaged or stolen... Shareholders' recourse against the Trust, the Trustee and the Sponsor, under New York law, the Custodian, under English law, and any subcustodians under the law governing their custody operations is limited. (p. 11)
- The Trust does not insure its gold. The Custodian maintains insurance with regard to its business on such terms and conditions as it considers appropriate which does not cover the full amount of gold held in custody. The Trust is not a beneficiary of any such insurance and does not have the ability to dictate the existence, nature or amount of coverage. Therefore, Shareholders cannot be assured that the Custodian will maintain adequate insurance or any insurance with respect to the gold held by the Custodian on behalf of the Trust. In addition, the Custodian and the Trustee do not require any direct or indirect subcustodians to be insured or bonded with respect to their custodial activities or in respect of the gold held by them on behalf of the Trust. Consequently, a loss may be suffered with

respect to the Trust's gold which is not covered by insurance and for which no person is liable in damages. (p. 11)

- The liability of the Custodian is limited under the agreements between the Trustee and the Custodian which establish the Trust's custody arrangements, or the Custody Agreements. Under the Custody Agreements, the Custodian is only liable for losses that are the direct result of its own negligence, fraud or willful default in the performance of its duties. (p. 11)

- If the Trust's gold bars are lost, damaged, stolen or destroyed under circumstances rendering a party liable to the Trust, the responsible party may not have the financial resources sufficient to satisfy the Trust's claim. (p. 12)

- Because neither the Trustee nor the Custodian oversees or monitors the activities of subcustodians who may temporarily hold the Trust's gold bars until transported to the Custodian's London vault, failure by the subcustodians to exercise due care in the safekeeping of the Trust's gold bars could result in a loss to the Trust. (p. 12)

- The Custodian does not undertake to monitor the performance by subcustodians of their custody functions or their selection of further subcustodians. The Trustee does not undertake to monitor the performance of any subcustodian. Furthermore, the Trustee may have no right to visit the premises of any subcustodian for the purposes of examining the Trust's gold bars or any records maintained by the subcustodian, and no subcustodian will be obligated to cooperate in any review the Trustee may wish to conduct of the facilities, procedures, records or creditworthiness of such subcustodian. (p. 13)

- Gold held in the Trust's unallocated gold account and any Authorized Participant's unallocated gold account will not be segregated from the Custodian's assets. If the Custodian becomes insolvent, its assets may not be adequate to satisfy a claim by the Trust or any Authorized Participant. (p. 13)

GLD is the largest gold bullion ETF with gold bullion with a stated value of $26.8 billion as of February 8, 2016. However, provisions in the prospectus lack sufficient safety as an investment vehicle.

iShares® Silver Trust (SLV)

The iShares® Silver Trust (SLV) is a trust designed to issue shares in exchange for silver bullion and distribute silver bullion in exchange for a minimum basket size of 50,000 shares. As of March 28, 2016, the Trust had net assets of $5.0 billion. The sponsor is iShares Delaware Trust Sponsor, LLC, a subsidiary of BlackRock, Inc. Bank of New York Mellon is the Trustee, and JPMorgan Chase Bank, London branch, is the Custodian of the Trust. Only registered broker-dealers that become authorized participants by entering into a contract with the Sponsor and the Trustee may purchase or redeem Baskets.

The most recent SLV prospectus is dated November 10, 2015. It is in stark contrast to the prospectus provisions of GLD. Based upon the provisions in the SLV prospectus, the Trustee and Custodian have better internal controls to prevent the loss of physical bullion bars, although the provision for insurance could be stronger. Two excerpts from the SLV prospectus follow:

- The Custodian may keep the Trust's silver at locations in England, New York, or with the consent of the Trustee and the Sponsor, in other places. The Custodian may, at its own expense and risk, use subcustodians to discharge its obligations to the Trust under the Custodian Agreement. The Custodian has agreed that it will only retain subcustodians if they agree to grant to the Trustee and the independent registered public accounting firm of the Trust access to records and inspection rights similar to those granted by JPMorgan Chase Bank N.A., London branch, in its agreement with the Trustee. The Custodian will remain responsible to the Trustee for any silver held by any subcustodian appointed by the Custodian to the same extent as if such silver were held by the Custodian itself. (p. 26–27)

- The Custodian has agreed to maintain insurance in support of its custodial obligations under the Custodian Agreement, including covering any loss of silver. The Custodian has the right to reduce, cancel or allow to expire without replacement this insurance coverage, provided that it gives prior written notice to the Trustee. In the case of a cancellation or expiration with replacement, the required notice must be at least 30 days prior to the last day of coverage. The insurance is held for the benefit of the Custodian, not for the benefit of the Trust or the Trustee, and the Trustee may not submit a claim under the insurance maintained by the Custodian. (p. 27)

Sprott Physical Gold Trust (PHYS) and Sprott Physical Silver Trust (PSLV)

Sprott Asset Management LP in Canada sponsors and manages the Sprott Physical Gold Trust (PHYS) and the Sprott Physical Silver Trust (PSLV). Both trusts have dual listings in the US and Canada. PHYS and PSLV allow unitholders to tender shares to the Transfer Agent for delivery of physical bullion. The minimum amount of gold and silver that can be delivered in exchange for the Sprott trust units is much smaller than the minimum amounts required for GLD or SLV.

PHYS is a trust established to hold substantially all of its assets in physical gold bullion. Unitholders have the ability, on a monthly basis, to redeem their units for physical gold bullion for a redemption price equal to 100% of the net asset value less redemption and delivery expenses. Redemption requests must be for amounts that are at least equivalent in value to one London Good Delivery bar (a single bar is between 350 and 430 troy ounces of gold).

PSLV is a trust established to hold substantially all of its assets in physical silver bullion. Unitholders have the ability, on a monthly basis, to redeem their units for physical silver bullion for a redemption price equal to 100% of the net asset value less redemption and delivery expenses. Redemption requests must be for amounts that are at least equivalent in value to ten London Good Delivery bars (a single bar is between 750 and 1,100 troy ounces of silver).

According to the most recent prospectuses for PHYS (dated February 25, 2010) and PSLV (dated October 28, 2010), there are some common features:

- Storage at the Royal Canadian Mint—Bullion is stored on a fully allocated basis at the Royal Canadian Mint, a Canadian Crown corporation which acts as an agent of the Canadian Government. The Mint will bear the risk of loss or damage to bullion in its custody. The bullion will be subject to a physical count by a representative of the Manager periodically on a spot-inspection basis as well as subject to audit procedures by the Trust's external auditors on at least an annual basis. (PHYS p. 2 and PSLV p. 2)
- RBC Dexia (Trustee), the Royal Canadian Mint (Custodian), and other service providers engaged by the Trust maintain such insurance as they deem appropriate with respect to their respective business and their positions as custodian, trustee or otherwise of the trust. Unitholders cannot be assured that any of the aforementioned parties will maintain any insurance with respect to the Trust's assets held or the services that such parties provide to the Trust and, if they maintain insurance, that such insurance is sufficient to satisfy any losses incurred by them in respect of their relationship with the Trust. In addition, none of the Trust's service providers is required to include the Trust as a named beneficiary of any such insurance policies that are purchased. Accordingly, the Trust will have to rely on the efforts of the service providers to recover from their insurer compensation for

any losses incurred by the Trust in connection with such arrangements. (PHYS p. 13 and PSLV p. 17)

Provisions in the prospectus appear to be adequate for PHYS and PSLV as investment vehicles. Although the statement regarding insurance could be stronger, the custodian is an agency of the Canadian government.

Central Fund of Canada Limited (CEF)

The Central Fund of Canada Limited (CEF) has a dual listing in Canada and the United States. It invests substantially all its assets in both gold and silver bullion. As of February 10, 2016, it had 63.4% of its total assets invested in gold bullion and 36.6% invested in silver bullion. Bullion holdings and bank vault security are inspected twice annually by directors and/or officers of Central Fund. On every occasion, inspections are required to be performed in the presence of external auditors and bank personnel. CEF's expense ratio is relatively low at 0.38% of assets for the most recent fiscal year ending October 31, 2015.

CEF does not allow the redemption of shares for physical bullion. This is in contrast to GLD, SLV, PHYS, and PSLV, which do allow the tendering of shares for bullion, although in minimum amounts that are beyond the capability of many investors. The bank may only release any portion of CEF's physical bullion holdings upon receipt of an authorizing resolution from CEF's Board of Directors. Consequently, CEF sold at an average discount to net asset value of 8.5% in 2015. During 2006 through 2012, CEF usually sold at a premium to net asset value.

Sprott Asset Management LP completed a hostile takeover of CEF's affiliated fund, Central Gold Trust, by merging it with PHYS in January 2016. In press releases and court filings, it has indicated its interest in merging CEF with PHYS and PSLV, which would reduce the discount to net asset value.

Below are some provisions from the most recent CEF prospectus dated November 1, 2012:

- All of the gold and silver bullion owned by Central Fund is stored on an unencumbered and allocated basis in the treasury vaults of the Canadian Imperial Bank of Commerce ("the Bank") in segregated safekeeping. (p. 21)
- The bullion is partially insured by Central Fund. While insurance is carried by the Bank, there is no assurance that such insurance is sufficient to satisfy any losses incurred by the Bank in respect of its relationship with Central Fund. In addition, Central Fund is not named beneficiary under such insurance and would have to rely on the Bank's efforts to recover its losses. Should such losses be found to be the fault of the Bank, recovery might be limited to the value of the gold and silver bullion at the time the loss is discovered. (p. 21)

Prospectus provisions appear adequate for investment, although the insurance provision could be stronger.

Tax Considerations

Under current law, the sale of shares or units of precious metals bullion ETFs that are domiciled in the United States (GLD and SLV) are subject to taxation as collectibles. If the holding period is longer than one year, gains are taxed at a maximum rate of 28% rather than the 20% rate applicable to most other long-term capital gains.

Precious metal ETFs that are domiciled in Canada (PHYS, PSLV, and CEF) are considered to be passive foreign investment companies (PFIC) for US federal income tax purposes. If a timely and valid qualified electing fund (QEF) election is made, any gains realized on the sale of shares may be taxable as long-term capital gains—at a maximum rate of 20% compared to the long-term capital gains tax rate of 28% on collectibles. See IRS Form 8621 instructions and/or a tax advisor for further information.

Conclusion

During a period of time when the four largest central banks (Federal Reserve, European Central Bank, Bank of Japan, and People's Bank of China) have adopted very aggressive monetary policies, investors should consider an allocation of a portion of their investment portfolio to gold and silver bullion ETFs and closed-end funds or physical coins and bars. The safety of the custodial facilities, insurance, taxes, and other considerations should be reviewed prior to purchase.

References

"Ask the Expert—Ted Butler—August 21, 2015." http://www.sprott-money.com/blog/ted-butler-coming-end-of-august-2015.html

"Comex on the Edge? Paper Gold 'Dilution' Hits a Record 124 for Every Ounce of Physical." 8/3/2015. http://www.zerohedge.com/news/2015-08-03/comex-edge-deliverable-gold-drops-record-low-124-ounces-paper-every-ounce-physical

"The Development and Opening of China's Gold Market—A Speech delivered by Xu Luode, Chairman of the Shanghai Gold Exchange, at the LBMA Bullion Market Forum in Singapore on 25 June, 2014." LBMA Alchemist, pages 6–8, issue 75, October 2014. https://live-bullioninternati.netdna-ssl.com/blogs/koos-jansen/wp-content/uploads/2015/02/Alchemist-75-Xu-Luode-Singapore.pdf

Roberts, Paul Craig and Dave Kranzler. "Supply and Demand in the Gold and Silver Futures Market." July 27, 2015. http://www.paulcraigroberts.org/2015/07/27/supply-demand-gold-silver-futures-markets-paul-craig-roberts-dave-kranzler/

Central Fund of Canada Short Form Base Shelf Prospectus, November 1, 2012. http://www.centralfund.com/prospectus/2012%20

Prospectus/CFOC%20-%20Final%20Base%20Shelf%20 Prospectus%20dated%20Nov%20%201%202012.pdf

Central Fund of Canada Annual Report, October 31, 2015. http:// www.centralfund.com/annualreport/CFOC%202015%20 AR%2010%20DEC%2015%20-%20FINAL.pdf

Hewitt, Mike. "Fate of Paper Money." June 29, 2008. http://www. safehaven.com/article/10637/fate-of-paper-money

IRS Instructions for Form 8621 (revised December 2015)— Information Return by a Shareholder of a Passive Foreign Investment Company or Qualified Electing Fund. https:// www.irs.gov/pub/irs-pdf/i8621.pdf

iShares Silver Trust Prospectus, November 10, 2015. https://www. ishares.com/us/library/stream-document?stream=reg&product=I-SLV&shareClass=NA&documentId=925420&iframeUrlOverride=/us/literature/prospectus/p-ishares-silver-trust-prospectus-12-31.pdf

SPDR Gold Trust (GLD) Prospectus dated July 17, 2015. https:// www.spdrs.com/library-content/public/SPDR_GOLD%20 TRUST_PROSPECTUS.pdf

Sprott Physical Gold Trust Prospectus, February 25, 2010. http:// sprottphysicalbullion.com/media/1341/sprottphysical-goldtrustprospectus-us.pdf

Sprott Physical Silver Trust Prospectus, October 28, 2010. http:// sprottphysicalbullion.com/media/1397/sprott-physical-silver-trust-prospectus-us.pdf

World Gold Council. http://www.gold.org/supply-and-demand

CHAPTER 11

Investment Funds at a Discount

> The most common cause of low prices is pessimism—sometimes pervasive, sometimes specific to a company or industry. We want to do business in such an environment, not because we like pessimism but because we like the prices it produces.
>
> —Warren Buffett,
> CEO of Berkshire Hathaway

Types of Investment Funds

There are several types of investment funds. Investment funds available to the general public include mutual funds, exchange-traded funds, and closed-end funds. Accredited investors also have access to hedge funds and other types of private placements that may target specific types of investments such as venture capital. In this chapter, we will discuss only investment funds available to the general public.

Most people are familiar with the open-end fund, commonly referred to as a mutual fund. The number of shares of a mutual fund will increase or decrease, depending on whether the fund has net sales or redemptions. An investor who wishes to purchase shares will buy at a price equal to the net asset value (or NAV) if it is a no-load fund. Net asset value is the market value of the fund's portfolio divided by the number of shares in the fund. If it is a load fund, investors will buy at a price equal to the net asset value plus a sales charge. When investors wish to redeem their shares, they notify the fund and receive the net asset value per share less any redemption fees.

Exchange-traded funds (ETFs) trade on a stock exchange throughout the day, unlike mutual funds, which trade based upon a calculation of net asset value at the end of the trading day. ETFs generally trade at prices that are small deviations from their net asset values during the trading day. Authorized participants are large broker-dealers that have agreements with ETF sponsors to exchange shares of an ETF for baskets of securities. The authorized broker-dealers may purchase and redeem ETF shares only in large blocks called creation units. The ability of ETFs to trade in close proximity to their net asset values relies upon the arbitrage activity of the authorized participants.

Many investors are not familiar with closed-end funds even though they often allow investors an opportunity to buy a portfolio of investments for less than the net asset value. Closed-end funds are issued through an initial public offering. The investors who purchase through the initial public offering will buy at an offering price that exceeds the net asset value. The difference is the underwriting discount, which goes to the securities firms that sell the fund. If an investor wishes to buy or sell shares of the fund after the public offering, they must do so by placing an order on an exchange, such as the New York Stock Exchange. After the public offering, stock brokerage firms are less enthusiastic about selling closed-end funds because commissions are lower than underwriting discounts. Without anyone actively marketing them, closed-end funds eventually may trade at a discount to net asset value. While this may be bad news for the original investors, it creates an opportunity for those who purchase closed-end funds at a discount to net asset value.

Table 11-1 A Comparison of Open-End and Closed-End Fund Characteristics

Characteristics	Open-End	Closed-End
Number of shares outstanding	Constantly changing	Set at initial offering and remains fixed
Public offering	Continuous	One time
Redemption by issuer?	Yes	No
Redemption Price	Net asset value (sometimes less a redemption fee)	Not redeemable by issuer
Where shares are bought and sold	From the investment company, underwriter, or dealer	On an exchange or over-the-counter
Relation of purchase price to net asset value	Purchase price = net asset value + sales charge (none if a no-load fund)	Set by supply and demand. Price may exceed the net asset value (trading at a premium) or may be less than the net asset value (trading at a discount).
Buying or selling costs	For load funds, there is a sales charge on the purchase. For no-load funds, there is no sales charge, but brokers may charge a transaction fee. There may be redemption fees upon the sale.	For both purchases and sales, there is a transaction fee or commission on the trade.

Source: Robert G. Kahl, CFA

The Advantage of Closed-End Funds at a Discount

Assuming that a closed-end fund has desirable holdings and meets other purchase criteria, if it is purchased when the probability is high that the discount will decrease, investment performance can be enhanced. The historical range of the market price discount or premium to net asset value for closed-end funds can be found on Morningstar.com or CEFA.com.

At the end of February 2016, Tri-Continental Corporation (symbol TY) sold at a discount to net asset value of 15.9%. TY is a large closed-end fund with net assets of $1.4 billion and an operating expense ratio of 0.69%. TY invests primarily in US stocks (70% as of February 2016), with an emphasis on large-cap stocks. It also holds some preferred stock and convertible securities. Its largest holdings as of February 2016 are Apple, Cisco, Philip Morris, Johnson & Johnson, JPMorgan Chase, Verizon, Home Depot, Intel, and Pfizer. TY has performed favorably in comparison to a blended benchmark during the last five years after a management change. Nevertheless, the range of the discount to net asset value during the last five years for TY has been between 12.8% and 16.3%. According to Morningstar, during the 2008 calendar year, the range of the discount to net asset value was 4.3% to 12.7%. The discount to net asset value now appears high given the portfolio holdings, performance, and expense ratio.

The Templeton Global Income Fund (GIM) invests in fixed-income securities outside of the United States and uses currency forward contracts to limit foreign currency exposure. As of December 31, 2015, it had 81% of its currency exposure in US dollars. As of the end of February 2016, it sold at a discount to net asset value of 13.3%. From 2011 through the first half of 2013, GIM regularly sold at a premium to net asset value. GIM does not use leverage and has a weighted average duration of less than one year. As of February 2016, it has an estimated yield of 3.84% when you exclude the portion of the distribution attributable to capital gains or return of capital. The illustration below demonstrates how income can be increased compared to an open-end (mutual) fund with the same holdings and operating expense ratio. If interest rates and the discount to net asset value are high enough, it is possible to have a yield on a closed-end fund that exceeds the yield of the underlying securities in the portfolio.

Table 11-2 Three Alternative Fixed Income Investments Using Templeton Global Income Fund as an Example—2/4/2016

	Individual Bonds	Open-End Fund	Closed-End Fund
Yield of bonds	4.14%	4.14%	4.14%
Operating expenses		0.73%	0.73%
Net income based upon NAV		3.41%	3.41%
Discount to NAV			11.21%
Price as a % of NAV			88.79%
Net income based upon price			3.84%

Source: Robert G. Kahl, CFA and CEFA.com

Use of Leverage by Closed-End Funds

Some closed-end funds use leverage to increase their net investment income. The Investment Company Act of 1940 limits the issuance of preferred shares to a maximum of 50% and debt issuance to a maximum of 33.33% of total assets. Both preferred shares and debt create claims that are senior to the claims of common shareholders. Closed-end funds are more likely to use leverage than open-end funds because they are not subject to share redemptions that could result in the forced sale of securities.

Debt issuance at low short-term rates in order to enhance yields is common among tax-exempt closed-end funds. Leverage has a positive impact on yield as long as the fund can borrow at interest rates that are lower than the yield of securities that the fund owns. Morningstar.com, CEFA.com, and investment company websites and literature show the amount of leverage being used by a closed-end fund.

Leverage increases the volatility of potential returns for common shareholders. Investors should consider the price volatility of the securities within a closed-end fund and the terms of borrowing before they make a purchase decision. A tax-exempt closed-end fund that is buying investment grade municipal bonds will have a lower expected volatility than a fund that holds high-yield bonds or foreign bonds denominated in local currency.

The Anderson Study

Seth Copeland Anderson conducted a comprehensive study on closed-end fund trading strategies. The results were classified into three different time periods. In the study, seventeen funds representing approximately 85% of the assets of all closed-end equity funds were included. The funds differed in size, investment objectives, and length of time included in each period. Nine of the funds included in the sample were characterized by diversified portfolios. Eight of the funds had specialized portfolios.

Mr. Anderson created portfolios of closed-end funds based upon the size of the discount to net asset value. Initially, each portfolio was worth $100,000, equally distributed among those funds that met the criterion for inclusion in the portfolio by selling at a discount greater than the prescribed amount. Portfolios were adjusted on the basis of trading rules—shares were purchased when the discount reached a predetermined level and sold when the discount narrowed by a given amount. The table below summarizes the results of the study.

As the table will indicate, each of the buy-and-sell point strategies for all funds provided higher returns than an investor would have received from the S&P 500 during the three periods.

On the subject of risk, Mr. Anderson concluded: "The weekly returns associated with the strategies were alternately more and less variable than the returns from investing in the S&P 500. Thus, if standard deviation of return is a proxy for risk, the results fail to confirm that an investor had to accept significantly more risk for a larger return."

Table 11-3 Anderson Study Results

Discount from net asset value when:		Performance Results			Cumulative Gain Per $1	Annual Geometric Average
Purchased	Sold	7/65–12/69	1/70–12/76	1/77–8/84		
5%	0%	+114%	+105%	+260%	15.79	15.5%
10	5	+129	+110	+262	17.41	16.1%
15	10	+147	+104	+334	21.87	17.5%
20	10	+136	+83	+387	21.03	17.2%
20	15	+135	+126	+448	29.10	19.2%
25	10	+171	+61	+404	21.99	17.5%
25	15	+123	+86	+387	20.20	17.0%
30	15	+49	+98	+344	13.10	14.4%
Buy and hold (no trading)		+86	+51	+273	10.47	13.0%
S & P 500 Index		+25	+49	+126	4.21	7.8%

Mergers of Closed-End Funds

Closed-end funds are sometimes merged with mutual funds managed by the same investment company. When shares of a closed-end fund are exchanged for shares of a mutual fund, it is invariably based upon the net asset value of both funds. This exchange process eliminates the discount to net asset value for the closed-end fund shareholders.

There are a number of reasons that an investment company may want to merge a closed-end fund into a mutual fund. If a closed-end fund sells at a large discount to net asset value for an extended period of time, the board of directors may be subject to pressure by investors to do something to reduce the discount. Closed-end funds cannot increase their assets (and management fees for the investment company) by selling additional shares on a daily basis like a mutual fund; they must sell additional shares through a secondary offering. Investment companies may also realize efficiencies by merging a closed-end fund into a mutual fund that has a similar strategy.

In July 2015, Transamerica Income Shares (TAI), a closed-end fund, and Transamerica Flexible Income, an open-end fund, announced that each fund's board of directors had approved a plan to merge TAI into Transamerica Flexible Income. The board recommendations were subject to shareholder approval, and the merger was finalized in December 2015. TAI had been selling at a discount to net asset value of approximately 10% prior to the merger. After the initial announcement, the price of TAI increased, and the discount to net asset value declined to about 2%. The discount to net asset value was eliminated when the merger was consummated with the exchange of shares based upon net asset value.

In January 2016, the Sprott Physical Gold Trust (PHYS) successfully completed a hostile merger of the Central Gold Trust (GTU) into PHYS. GTU was a closed-end fund that held gold bullion and was selling at a discount to net asset value of approximately 7% prior to the takeover attempt. PHYS is an ETF that allows unitholders to redeem shares for physical gold bullion bars, subject to a minimum size of 350–430 troy ounces (London good delivery bar specifications). Consequently, the market price of PHYS tracks closely the net asset value, and GTU shareholders had an incentive to approve the merger since their shares frequently sold at a single-digit discount to net asset value.

Distributions

Some closed-end funds adopt policies of high distributions that exceed net investment income. Net investment income consists of dividends, interest, and realized capital gains less operating expenses of the fund. Distributions in excess of net investment income represent a return of capital.

The purpose of high distribution policies is to reduce the discount to net asset value as funds with high yields are generally more attractive to investors. While high distributions may not eliminate a discount to net asset value for a closed-end fund, they represent a partial liquidation at net asset value, which should enhance returns over time.

Conclusion

Closed-end funds are likely to improve investment returns if they are purchased at a discount to net asset value that is high relative to its historical range and sold when the discount is reduced. Investors considering leverage funds should review the terms of borrowing and the potential price volatility of portfolio holdings.

References

Closed-End Fund Center. www.cefa.com

Anderson, Seth Copeland, "Closed-end Funds Versus Market Efficiency." *Journal of Portfolio Management*, Fall, 1986.

Investment Company Institute. "Frequently Asked Questions about Closed-End Funds and Their Use of Leverage." https://www.ici.org/pubs/faqs/faqs_closed_end

Nuveen Investments. "Understanding Leverage in Closed-End Funds." http://www.nuveen.com/Home/Documents/Default.aspx?fileId=59138

CHAPTER 12

The US Financial System

The lesson of history is that you do not get a sustained economic recovery as long as the financial system is in crisis.

—Ben Bernanke,
chairman of the Federal Reserve,
2006–2014

Commercial Banks

Commercial banks serve as an intermediary between households and organizations that deposit money and households and organizations that borrow money. Banks normally have a positive spread between the interest rate that they earn on loans and marketable securities and the interest rate they pay to depositors and other creditors.

The management of risk is of critical importance at banks. Banks attempt to match the duration of their assets and liabilities as much as possible. Otherwise, when interest rates rise, their cost of funds on typically shorter duration liabilities will adjust upward faster than interest on longer-duration assets. Banks also attempt to match the currency of their assets and liabilities. This is not an issue for smaller banks, but it can be an issue for large international banks.

Table 12-1 Assets and Liabilities of Commercial Banks in the United States
March 2016—Not Seasonally Adjusted

Assets	$ Billions	% of Total Assets
Securities		
Treasury and agency	2,260.2	14.4%
Other securities	892.5	5.7%
Subtotal	3,152.7	20.0%
Loans and Leases		
Commercial and industrial	2,028.0	12.9%
Real estate	3,925.2	25.0%
Consumer	1,275.9	8.1%
Other loans	1,512.9	9.6%
Less allowance for losses	(106.9)	-0.7%
Subtotal	8,635.1	54.9%
Interbank loans	59.5	0.4%
Cash assets	2,514.8	16.0%
Trading assets	211.4	1.3%
Other assets	1,153.1	7.3%
Total Assets	15,726.6	100.0%
Liabilities		
Deposits		
Large time deposits	1,682.7	10.7%
Other	9,468.5	60.2%
Subtotal	11,151.2	70.9%
Borrowings	1,933.7	12.3%
Trading Liabilities	225.7	1.4%
Net due to related foreign offices	318.3	2.0%
Other liabilities	395.4	2.5%
Total Liabilities	14,024.3	89.2%
Residual (Owners' Equity)	1,702.3	10.8%

Source: www.federalreserve.gov/releases/h8/current

120

Loan quality is another important consideration. During recessions, which appear to be inevitable, nonperforming loans rise and expenses associated with loan write-offs increase.

Table 12-1 shows the total assets and liabilities of all commercial banks in the United States. Total assets of all commercial banks in the United States were equal to $15.6 trillion as of the end of January 2016. Cash assets include deposits at Federal Reserve Banks. Treasury and agency securities are a second source of liquidity since these types of securities are more marketable and have lower transaction costs. The fair value of derivatives is included in trading assets and/or liabilities.

FDIC Insurance

Depositor confidence in the US banking system relies upon deposit insurance provided by the Federal Deposit Insurance Corporation (FDIC), which was created in 1933 in response to bank runs during the Great Depression. Since the FDIC was established in 1933, no depositor has lost a penny of FDIC-insured funds. There are eight distinct ownership categories that are insured separately at each bank up to the insurance limit. Each co-owner of a joint account is insured up to the insurance limit.

Confidence in FDIC-insured deposits remains high, and they are generally considered to be "risk-free." The FDIC claims on their website that FDIC insurance is backed by the "full faith and credit of the United States government" based on the clause in the "Sense of Congress" paragraph of Title IX of the Competitive Equality Banking Act of 1987 (CEBA). However, according to an advisory opinion provided by Alan J. Kaplan, legal counsel for the FDIC in November 1987:

> While any final conclusion on this matter rests
> with the Attorney General of the United States
> and ultimately with the courts, it is our opin-

ion that Title IX of CEBA merely represents an expression of the intent of Congress to support the FDIC's deposit insurance fund should the need arise. Title IX does not change any existing underlying law. It does not amend the Federal Deposit Insurance Act, nor does it or any other provision of CEBA alter the method by which the FDIC is funded. The FDIC continues to receive no government appropriations, and its funding continues to consist entirely of its income obtained from insurance assessments and from the return on investments made in government securities. In addition, the FDIC's statutory authority to borrow up to $3.0 billion from the Treasury remains unchanged.

During the recent financial crisis, the FDIC had fund balances at the end of 2009 and 2010 of negative $20.86 billion and $7.35 billion, respectively. No additional funds were provided to the FDIC by Congress during the financial crisis. Insurance assessments were increased for member institutions and the FDIC gradually improved its financial position.

To alleviate concerns about bank deposits during the most recent financial crisis, the bank deposit insurance limit was temporarily increased in October 2008 from $100,000 to $250,000. The Dodd-Frank Wall Street Reform and Consumer Protection Act, which was signed into law in July 2010, made the higher limit permanent.

As of December 31, 2014, the FDIC Deposit Insurance Fund (DIF) had a positive fund balance of $62.8 billion. The DIF is 1.0% of $6.2 trillion of insured deposits that it covers at over 6,500 institutions. The FDIC also managed nearly 500 active receiverships with total assets of $29.7 billion at year-end 2014. The FDIC's goal, which is mandated by statute, is to exceed a ratio of the DIF fund balance to insured deposits of 1.35% by September 2020.

Bail-Ins

After the financial crisis of 2008–2009, governments around the world realized that bailing out banks was beyond the resources of most governments due to high government debt levels and the size of the financial system relative to the various economies. Since then, legal frameworks for ensuring continuity of all critical services provided by banks without taxpayer assistance have been put in place by many countries to reduce risks to financial stability.

The Financial Stability Board (FSB) was established after the 2009 G-20 London summit as an international body that monitors and makes recommendations about the global financial system. The FSB is a successor to the Financial Stability Forum and consists of all G-20 countries, four other countries, and the European Commission. In October 2011, the FSB published its "Key Attributes of Effective Resolution Regimes for Financial Institutions" to provide guidance regarding the core elements to resolve potential instability of financial institutions "without taxpayer exposure to loss from solvency support." In October 2014, the FSB updated its key attributes to provide additional guidance, including sector-specific information.

Included in the FSB's key attributes are powers to "convert into equity or other instruments of ownership of the firm under resolution… all or parts of unsecured and uninsured creditor claims in a manner that respects the hierarchy of claims in liquidation." This approach was utilized during the March 2013 banking crisis in Cyprus. Bank accounts in excess of 100,000 euros were partially converted to bank shares of questionable value.

In December 2012, the FDIC and the Bank of England (BOE) issued a joint working paper entitled "Resolving Globally Active, Systemically Important, Financial Institutions." The Dodd-Frank Act provided the enabling legislation to implement the recommendations of the FSB. Title I of the Dodd-Frank Act requires each globally active systemically important financial institution (GSIFI) to periodically submit to the FDIC and the Federal Reserve a resolution plan that must address the company's plans for its rapid and orderly resolution under the US Bankruptcy Code. Title II of the Dodd-Frank Act provides the FDIC with additional powers to resolve SIFIs by establishing the orderly liquidation authority (OLA). The FDIC/BOE working paper describes the authority:

> Under the OLA, the FDIC may be appointed receiver for any U.S. financial company that meets specified criteria, including being in default or in danger of default, and whose resolution under the U.S. Bankruptcy Code (or other relevant insolvency process) would likely create systemic instability. Title II requires that the losses of any financial company placed into receivership will not be borne by taxpayers, but by common and preferred stockholders, debt holders, and other unsecured creditors, and that management responsible for the condition of the financial company will be replaced. Once appointed receiver for a failed financial company, the FDIC would be required to carry out a resolution of the company in a manner that mitigates risk to financial stability and minimizes moral hazard. Any costs borne by the U.S. authorities in resolving the institution not paid from proceeds of the resolution will be recovered from the industry.

Thus, many have described this as a bail-in process where creditor liabilities are involuntarily converted to bank capital rather than a bail-out process where funds are provided by taxpayers.

Derivatives

A financial derivative is a contract between two parties that derives its value and price from an underlying asset, index, or interest rate. Derivatives may be used to hedge an existing market exposure to reduce risk or as highly leveraged instruments to increase exposure to a particular facet of the financial markets. The notional amount of a derivative contract is the nominal or face amount that is used to calculate payments made on that contract. The payments exchanged between parties may be a small or larger percentage of the notional value of the contract, depending on the volatility of the underlying asset, the terms of the derivatives contract, and the length of time to expiration. The most common types of derivatives are futures, forwards, options, and swaps.

Futures contracts are between parties that agree to buy or sell an asset for a priced agreed upon today with delivery and payment occurring at a future delivery date. Contracts are standardized and traded on a futures exchange. There are margin requirements for both parties that vary with the volatility of the price of the deliverable asset.

Forward contracts are non-standardized contracts between two parties to buy or sell an asset at a price agreed upon today with delivery and payment at a future date. Because they are not standardized contracts, they do not sell on an exchange.

Options are a type of contract that gives the buyer the right, but not the obligation, to buy or sell an asset at a specified price on or before a specified date. Options may be standardized and traded on an exchange or they may be nonstandardized and traded over-the-counter.

Swap agreements (swaps) are contracts in which two counterparties agree to exchange different cash flow streams. The swap agreement defines when the cash flows are to be paid and the way they are calculated. Unlike the other types of derivatives, the notional amount is not exchanged between counterparties. Swaps are settled in cash or collateral.

The global derivatives market has experienced exponential growth during the last three decades. The International Swap Dealers Association (ISDA) estimates that the total notional value of over-the-counter (OTC) and exchange-traded derivatives amounted to US$1.73 trillion in 1987. According to the Bank of International Settlements (BIS), the total notional value of OTC and exchange-traded derivatives amounted to US$615.1 trillion as of June 30, 2015. The BIS breakdown of the OTC market is in the table below.

Table 12-2 Global Over-the-Counter Derivatives Market June 30, 2015

	Billions of US Dollars	
	Notional Amount Outstanding	Gross Market Value
Foreign exchange	$ 74,519	$ 2,547
Interest rate	434,740	11,081
Equity-linked	7,545	606
Commodity	1,671	237
Credit default swaps	14,596	453
Unallocated	19,837	597
Totals	$ 552,908	$ 15,521

Source: Bank for International Settlements

The gross market value is the sum of the values of all outstanding derivatives contracts with either positive or negative replacement values based upon market prices on the reporting date. One firm's positive value on a contract should, in theory, be equal to the negative value on the same contract held by its counterparty. However, since OTC derivative contracts are not standardized and traded on an exchange, the counterparties may be using different methods for estimating fair market value.

According to the BIS, the notional value of global exchange-traded futures and options amount to US$62.2 trillion as of June 30, 2015—$61.8 trillion of this amount is related to interest rates, and the remainder is related to foreign exchange. The BIS does not have reliable information on the notional amount outstanding for exchange-traded equity-linked, commodity, and credit default swap derivatives.

According to the CIA's World Fact Book, the gross world product in nominal terms was US$78.3 trillion in 2014. Thus, the ratio of the notional value of derivatives outstanding identified by the BIS divided by the gross world product is 7.86, and most of the derivatives are concentrated in the European and American economies. The magnitude of the derivatives market clearly exceeds the requirements of nonfinancial businesses to hedge risk. A significant portion of derivatives activity appears to be leveraged speculation.

Table 12-3 Derivatives of Top Five US Financial/Bank Holding Companies Gross Notional Amount by Type, in Billions of US$ September 30, 2015

	Interest Rate	Foreign Exchange	Equity-Linked	Precious Metals	Credit	Other	Total
JPMorgan Chase & Co.	47,516	9,633	1,541	18	3,525	746	62,979
Citigroup Inc.	35,361	8,261	426	6	2,411	186	46,651
Goldman Sachs Group, Inc.	40,129	887	59	0	167	8	41,250
Bank of America Corp.	20,244	6,235	319	0	1,819	21	28,638
Wells Fargo & Co.	5,562	352	95	2	20	45	6,076
Totals	148,812	25,368	2,440	26	7,942	1,006	185,594

Source: Office of the Comptroller of the Currency

The derivatives exposure of the top-five US banks is shown in Table 12-3. There is a significant reduction in the use of derivatives between no. 4 Bank of America and no. 5 Wells Fargo. The total notional amount of derivatives of the top five US banks is US$185.6 trillion, which is 10.65 times US GDP. The derivatives books of the largest banks in the US are quite large relative to the size of their own balance sheets and the US economy.

Satyajit Das has over thirty years of experience in the derivatives market and is the author of two reference works on derivatives and risk management. His book *Traders, Guns & Money*, is an insider's view of the derivatives market. He writes the following about the potential for speculative use of derivatives:

> The derivatives industry uses several defences to the accusation that derivatives are speculative... Members of a congressional committee asked the chairman of a major American bank whether derivatives were speculative. He answered that derivatives were not inherently speculative although they could be used for speculation. If speculation was your objective then derivatives were an exceedingly efficient way to do it... In truth, a good chunk of the activity in the derivatives markets is driven by speculation. Part of it is obscured by semantics— the boundary between speculation and investment is always hazy. If you lost money you speculated. If you made money you were investing. Or was it the other way around?

Repo Market

The sale and repurchase agreement (repo) market is often referred to as the shadow banking system. Repos are short-term money market instruments used by institutional investors and nonfinancial firms that must store cash, earn some interest, and maintain short-term liquidity. Companies with large cash balances that exceed FDIC insurance limits often use the repo market as an alternative to bank deposits.

The repo market is large relative to the banking system. At the end of 2014, the Federal Reserve Bank of New York estimated the outstanding repo of its primary dealers (who may account for 90% of the US market) to be at US$4.6 trillion. The European repo market is equally large. The International Capital Market Association (IMCA) conducted a survey in December 2014 and estimated the size of the European repo market at 5.5 trillion euros.

In a repo transaction, a dealer sells securities for cash and agrees to buy the securities back at a predetermined price in the future—usually the next day. Reverse repo is the other side of the transaction—a firm agrees to buy securities and sell them back to the other party at a predetermined price. In essence, this type of transaction is a short-term collateralized loan. Most repo transactions are done on an overnight basis and renewed daily. Transactions that are for periods longer than one day are called term repo. Any interest received plus the change in accrued interest during the holding period represent interest income to the reverse repo party. Securities used as collateral in a repo transaction can be rehypothecated or reused as collateral in other transactions with other parties.

Ideally, repo collateral should be free of credit risk and highly liquid so that it can be easily sold for a predictable value in the event of default by the collateral-giver. In the US, approximately two-thirds of repo collateral consists of US Treasury securities. Government-guaranteed agency debt and agency mortgage-backed securities also make up a significant portion of repo collateral. There are some types of repo collateral that are more credit-sensitive and less liquid: corporate bonds, non-agency MBS, and structured products such as asset-backed securities (ABS) and collateralized debt obligations (CDO).

Gary Gorton and Andrew Metrick, economics professors at Yale University, argue that the financial crisis of 2007–2008 was the result of a repo market panic involving increasing repo haircuts (allowance for defaults or overcollateralization) and deleveraging. In the precrisis period, haircuts were zero for all asset classes used as repo collateral. Due to credit concerns on subprime and other structured products, repo market participants started requiring haircuts at the end of 2007, and the haircuts increased throughout 2008. By late 2008, subprime structured products could no longer be used as repo collateral while the haircut on non-subprime structured products reached 20%. The impact on investment grade corporate bonds was modest as haircuts went from zero to 2.5% by late 2008. As haircuts on certain types of securities increased, repo market participants sold them and substituted more acceptable collateral. Consequently, US Treasury and agency securities performed well, and credit spreads on non-agency mortgage backed securities and structured products widened dramatically.

Superior Credit Status of Derivatives and Repurchase Agreements

In an article published in the Stanford Law Review, Mark Roe, Professor at Harvard Law School, argues that the superpriority status of derivatives and repurchase agreements in the Bankruptcy Code weakens market discipline because counterparties know that they will likely be paid even if their derivatives or repo counterparty fails.

Normally, filing for bankruptcy has the following impact on a firm's creditors:

1. The code bars creditors from trying to collect debts due from the bankrupt.
2. Creditors who have been paid within ninety days before a bankruptcy filing must return those payments to the bankrupt, thereby benefiting all other creditors.
3. Ordinary creditors lack the right without court permission to set off as many of their own debts that are due to the debtor.
4. Bankrupt firms can recover prebankruptcy fraudulent conveyances, which arise when the debtor sells its own assets for less than fair value.

5. The code limits most creditors' rights to terminate contracts with the bankrupt firm.
6. Creditors cannot terminate their contracts with a bankrupt firm if the firm files to reorganize under chapter 11.

According to Professor Roe, each of these rules is reversed for creditor claims related to derivatives and repurchase agreements. Thus, there are really two sets of bankruptcy rules for creditors. Furthermore, code priorities that reduce risk for derivatives and repo counterparties raise risk for other creditors.

Derivatives contracts normally have contingent collateral posting requirements if the credit rating of a counterparty declines or the credit rating of existing collateral declines. For ordinary creditors, such additional collateral postings on the eve of bankruptcy would be a voidable preference and have to be returned. But the Bankruptcy Code's preference for derivatives allow such additional collateral postings. As additional collateral is posted, more default risk moves to parties who cannot, or will not, react contractually. Professor Roe writes: "Some are poorly positioned and too weakly informed to monitor the debtor's overall riskiness in general and its derivatives portfolio in particular. The new risk bearers are initially insurance policyholders, bank depositors, ordinary commercial paper buyers, and similar players who are often not well informed about the derivatives market."

Federal Reserve System

The Federal Reserve System (Fed) was created by the enactment of the Federal Reserve Act on December 23, 1913, to provide a central bank for the United States. The three original key objectives for monetary policy in the Federal Reserve Act were the following: (1) maximum employment, (2) stable prices, and (3) moderate long-term interest rates. Its responsibilities have since expanded to include supervising and regulating banks, maintaining stability of the financial system and providing financial services to depository institutions, the US government, and foreign official institutions. The Fed also conducts research and releases publications on the economy and monetary policy.

The Fed consists of twelve regional Federal Reserve Districts with banks in major cities, many member banks that provide capital, a board of governors appointed by the president of the United States, and a Federal Open Market Committee to oversee open market operations of the Fed. The member banks receive a 6% dividend on their capital provided to the Fed and any remaining profits are paid to the US Treasury.

Since the 2008–2009 financial crisis, the Fed has also elevated the prices of financial assets by purchasing fixed-income securities, including agency mortgage-backed securities on a much larger scale than it has in the past. This policy, referred to as quantitative easing (or QE), has been justified by an aggressive interpretation of the three original key objectives and a new objective of increasing asset prices (the wealth effect) with the goal of improving consumer sentiment and spending. The Fed's balance sheet has undergone a massive shift as a result.

As Table 12-4 shows, Federal Reserve System assets increased from $893.8 billion at the end of 2007 to $4,486.3 billion as of February 10, 2016. There was a large increase in holdings of US Treasury securities while agency mortgage backed securities increased from zero to $1,744.2 billion. On the liabilities side of the balance sheet, there was also a huge increase in deposits held at Federal Reserve Banks. Deposits increased from $16.4 billion to $2,783.0 billion. The increase in deposits is the result of sales of Treasury securities and MBS by banks and other financial institutions to the Fed. Rather than being reinvested in similar securities, the proceeds of the sales have been held as deposits at the Fed. Effective December 16, 2008, the Fed began to pay interest of 0.25% on required and excess reserves at the Federal Reserve Banks. For reasons that are not entirely clear, banks have been willing to accept an interest rate of 0.25% on deposits at the Fed rather than invest in securities that offer a higher interest rate, albeit with more interest rate and credit risk.

Table 12-4 Federal Reserve System Balance Sheet Comparison

	12/26/2007 $US M	12/26/2007 % of Assets	2/10/2016 $US M	2/10/2016 % of Assets
Assets				
Gold certificate account	11,037	1.23%	11,037	0.25%
SDR certificate account	2,200	0.25%	5,200	0.12%
Coin	1,173	0.13%	2,006	0.04%
Securities				
US Treasury	754,612	84.43%	2,461,174	54.86%
Federal agency debt			31,318	0.70%
Repurchase agreements	42,500	4.75%		
Agency mortgage backed securities			1,744,180	38.88%
Unamortized premium and discounts - net			170,939	3.81%
Loans - term auction credit and other	24,535	2.74%	11	0.00%
Net portfolio holdings of Maiden Lane LLC			1,722	0.04%
Bank premises	2,128	0.24%	2,231	0.05%
Foreign currency denominated assets			20,458	0.46%
Other assets	55,633	6.22%	36,002	0.80%
Total Assets	893,818	100.00%	4,486,278	100.00%
Liabilities				
Federal Reserve notes	791,801	88.59%	1,373,926	30.63%
Reverse repurchase agreements	40,542	4.54%	282,372	6.29%
Deposits	16,358	1.83%	2,783,045	62.03%
Other liabilities	8,005	0.90%	7,423	0.17%
Total Liabilities	856,706	95.85%	4,446,766	99.12%
Total Capital	37,112	4.15%	39,512	0.88%

Source: Federal Reserve statistical releases H.4.1

The gold certificate account shown on the Fed's balance sheet represents 8,130 metric tonnes of gold at an official price of $42.2222 per troy ounce. The Gold Reserve Act of 1934 required the Fed to transfer ownership of all of its gold to the Department of the Treasury. In exchange, the US Treasury issued gold certificates to the Fed for the amount of gold transferred at the official price. Based on existing law, however, gold certificates do not give the Fed any right to redeem the certificates for gold.

A significant difference between the 12/26/2007 and 2/10/2016 balance sheets is the total capital of the Federal Reserve Banks. Capital did not increase as fast as assets in recent years, so the ratio of total capital-to-assets declined from 4.15% to 0.88%. Amounts shown on the Fed's balance sheet for securities are not current market values. Securities are shown at face or par value. Unamortized premiums and discounts are shown on a separate line. The assumption is that all securities will be held until maturity. Given the Fed's thin capitalization, marking their securities to current market prices could easily lead to a negative capital position.

Federal Government

The US government is the contingent funding source of last resort for the FDIC, the commercial banking system, the Federal Reserve System, and agencies such as Fannie Mae and Freddie Mac. As such, it is worthwhile to look at the current state of the US government finances. Figure 12-1 shows how US government revenues and expenditures have changed as a percentage of GDP since 1930. There was a dramatic increase in expenditures for World War II. Recently, there were large budget deficits during the years 2009 through 2012.

Figure 12-1

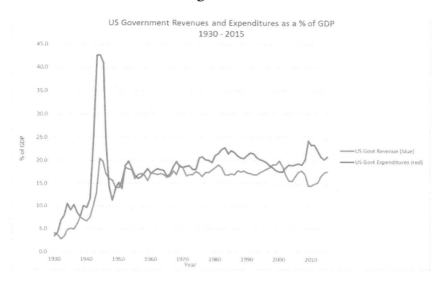

US Government Revenues and Expenditures as a % of GDP
1930 - 2015

Source: WhiteHouse.gov (Office of Management and Budget)

The cumulative effect of persistent US government budget deficits is shown in Figure 12-2 with a steady rise in federal government debt as a percentage of GDP to a level that has not been experienced since World War II. The Office of Management and Budget estimates that federal receipts as a percentage of GDP were 17.7% for fiscal year 2015. The federal debt-to-GDP ratio was 103.0%, or 5.85 times higher than federal receipts. If interest rates do not decline, higher government debt levels result in an increasing portion of government expenditures being dedicated to interest expense. Higher debt levels may also eventually lead to lower credit ratings and higher interest rates to compensate for higher default risk and currency risk.

Figure 12-2

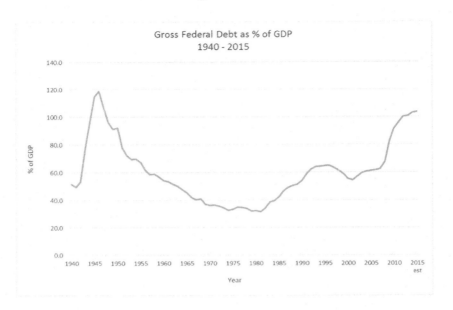

Source: WhiteHouse.gov (Office of Management and Budget)

The ability of the US government to raise income tax rates is limited somewhat by the additional layer of taxes from state and local governments. For fiscal year 2015, state and local government revenue was 16.6% of GDP. Total tax revenue (federal, state, and local) was 34.3% of GDP.

The United States is among the top ten most indebted countries of the world. Some of the other countries on the list have been in the news because of their precarious financial situation. Greece, Portugal, Ireland, and Spain were unable to repay or refinance their debt in recent years without the assistance of the European Central Bank and/or the International Monetary Fund. The economies of Japan and the United States are much larger, so it would be very difficult to design a bailout program for either country.

Table 12-5 Top-Ten Most Indebted Countries December 2015

Country	Debt/GDP
Japan	230.0%
Greece	179.0%
Italy	132.8%
Portugal	129.1%
Belgium	106.1%
United States	103.0%
Spain	100.7%
Singapore	99.3%
Ireland	98.4%
France	96.2%

Source: tradingeconomics.com

The Financial Report of the United States government for the fiscal year ending September 30, 2014 is prepared primarily on the basis of the Statement of Federal Financial Accounting Standards. Expenses are generally recognized when incurred. The status of social insurance programs is not reflected in the balance sheet but is shown as supplementary information. According to the supplementary information for fiscal year 2014, the estimated present value of net expenditures over a seventy-five-year time horizon of social insurance programs (Social Security, Medicare, Railroad Retirement, and Black Lung Disability Trust Fund) as of September 30, 2014, totaled $41.9 trillion (or 2.43 times 2014 GDP). Absent any changes to social insurance benefits and tax rates, it will be difficult to reduce the federal government's budget deficit in future years.

Conclusion

The capital ratios of US commercial banks and the FDIC appear to be adequate at this time. However, the five largest US commercial banks have derivative holdings that are very large relative to their capital base. Derivatives represent one potential source of financial instability in US financial markets due to the magnitude of derivatives contracts outstanding and their superpriority status in bankruptcy proceedings. A second source of financial instability is the repo market due to the size and opacity of the market, and changes in collateral requirements during times of financial stress.

Any response to financial crises by the Fed and the US government will likely be more limited in the future due to the current low capital ratio of the Fed and the relatively high debt level of the US government.

References

Adams, Stephen D. "Derivatives Safe Harbors in Bankruptcy and Dodd-Frank: A Structural Analysis." Harvard Law School. April 30, 2013. https://dash.harvard.edu/handle/1/10985175

Anderson, Ronald W., and Kenneth McKay. "Derivatives Markets." London School of Economics. March 2006 for inclusion in *Financial Markets and Institutions: A European Perspective* to be published by Oxford University Press. http://personal.lse.ac.uk/ANDERSOR/DM_2006_FEB_06_v2.pdf

Bank of International Settlements. www.bis.org

CIA World Factbook. https://www.cia.gov/library/publications/the-world-factbook/

Federal Deposit Insurance Corporation. www.fdic.gov

Federal Reserve System. www.federalreserve.gov

Federal Reserve Bank of St. Louis—Economic Research. https://research.stlouisfed.org/

Federal Reserve System. "Does the Federal Reserve Own or Hold Gold?" http://www.federalreserve.gov/faqs/does-the-federal-reserve-own-or-hold-gold.htm

Federal Deposit Insurance Corporation. "Resolving Globally Active, Systemically Important, Financial Institutions: A Joint Paper by the Federal Deposit Insurance Corporation and the Bank of England." December 10, 2012. https://www.fdic.gov/about/srac/2012/gsifi.pdf

Financial Report of the United States Government—Fiscal Year 2014. https://www.fiscal.treasury.gov/fsreports/rpt/finrep/fr/14frusg/FR_02252015_Final.pdf

Financial Stability Board. "Key Attributes of Effective Resolution Regimes for Financial Institutions." October 2011. http://www.financialstabilityboard.org/wp-content/uploads/r_111104cc.pdf?page_moved=1

Financial Stability Board. "Key Attributes of Effective Resolution Regimes for Financial Institutions." October 15, 2014. http://www.financialstabilityboard.org/wp-content/uploads/r_141015.pdf

GoldCore. "From Bail-Outs to Bail-Ins: Risks and Ramifications." November 2013. http://info.goldcore.com/guide-to-bank-deposit-bail-ins-risks-ramifications

Gorton, Gary and Andrew Metrick. "Haircuts." Federal Reserve Bank of St. Louis Review, November/December 2010, pp. 507–519. https://research.stlouisfed.org/publications/review/10/11/Gorton.pdf

International Capital Market Association. www.icmagroup.org

Kaplan, Alan J. "Advisory Opinion—Full Faith and Credit of U.S. Government behind the FDIC Deposit Insurance Fund, November 9, 1987." https://www.fdic.gov/regulations/laws/rules/4000-2660.html

Office of Management and Budget—historical tables. https://www.whitehouse.gov/omb/budget/Historicals

Office of the Comptroller of the Currency. OCC's Quarterly Report on Bank Trading and Derivatives Activities, Third Quarter

2015. http://www.occ.treas.gov/topics/capital-markets/financial-markets/trading/derivatives/dq315.pdf

Roe, Mark J. "The Derivatives Market's Payment Priorities as Financial Crisis Accelerator." Stanford Law Review, vol. 63, issue 3—March 2011. http://www.stanfordlawreview.org/print/article/derivatives-markets-payment-priorities-financial-crisis-accelerator

Sundaram, Rangarajan K. "Derivatives in Financial Market Development." International Growth Centre (IGC)—Working Paper, Stern School of Business, New York University, September 2012. http://www.theigc.org/wp-content/uploads/2015/02/Sundaram-2012-Working-Paper.pdf.

Trading Economics. www.tradingeconomics.com

US Government Revenue history compiled by Christopher Chantrill. http://www.usgovernmentrevenue.com/

Wikipedia. www.wikipedia.org

CHAPTER 13

Economics—Competing and Complementary Theories

By a continuing process of inflation, government can confiscate, secretly and unobserved, an important part of the wealth of their citizens. By this method they not only confiscate but they confiscate arbitrarily; and, while the process impoverishes many, it actually enriches some.

—John Maynard Keynes,
English economist

One of the great mistakes is to judge policies and programs by their intentions rather than their results.

—Milton Friedman, American economist

The purpose of this chapter is to provide an overview of some of the competing and complementary macroeconomic theories that often enter into political and economic policy debates. A basic understanding of these theories has become more important during our current era of high debt levels and "quantitative easing" monetary policies in major countries around the world.

Classical Economics

Adam Smith's book *The Wealth of Nations* was published in 1776 and is considered to be the foundation of classical economics. Smith's central point was that the wealth of nations was based upon trade. He used the metaphor of an "invisible hand" to illustrate that markets generally regulate themselves when free of coercion. Smith, however, was in favor of limited government intervention for education to subsidize school buildings, legally obliging subjects to attain certain educational levels and subsidizing fees payable by poor families. Smith and others redirected economics away from analysis of the ruler's personal interests to broader national interests.

Other classical economists include Jean-Baptiste Say, David Ricardo, and Thomas Malthus. Say argued in favor of competition and free trade. He is known for Say's law, or the law of markets, which states that aggregate production increases aggregate demand because producers will have more income to spend. David Ricardo is best known for his theory of comparative advantage that states that overall wealth is increased when people specialize in activities where they are most competitive. Thomas Malthus is best known for his writing about the limitations of population and economic growth.

Neoclassical Economics

Neoclassical economics together with Keynesian economics dominates mainstream economics today. There appears to be some difference of opinion on what constitutes neoclassical economics. E. Roy Weintraub, professor of economics at Duke University, believes that neoclassical economics has three basic assumptions:

1. People have rational preferences between outcomes that can be identified and associated with values.
2. Individuals maximize utility and firms maximize profits.
3. People act independently on the basis of full and relevant information.

On the basis of these assumptions, theories are derived about the allocation of resources and economic activity.

Keynes and the Abuse of His Theories

John Maynard Keynes was a British economist whose economic theories had a profound effect on government policies of the twentieth and twenty-first centuries. During the Great Depression, Keynes wrote three books: *Treatise on Money* (1930), *The Means to Prosperity* (1933), and *The General Theory of Employment, Interest and Money* (1936). Keynes challenged the widely accepted neoclassical theory that the market would naturally establish full employment equilibrium as workers accept lower wages so that employers could employ them and make a profit.

Keynes argued, contrary to most economists of his time, that capitalist economies were not inherently self-correcting. Declining wages and prices could lead to lower consumption, reduced investment, and an increase in the real burden of debtors due to deflation. While Keynes seems to acknowledge that the economy would eventually recover on its own, he believed that active government policies would result in a quicker recovery. He criticized the laissez-faire attitude of conventional economists when he wrote, "Economists set them too easy, too useless a task if in tempestuous seasons they can only tell us that when the storm is over the ocean is flat again."

Keynes advocated that governments engage in counter-cyclical public spending programs such as public works to stimulate aggregate demand (the sum of consumption and investment) in times of high unemployment. He believed that the economic benefits of such public spending programs would be magnified due to the multiplier effect as direct recipients of government payments generate other economic benefits. When an economy improves, Keynes believed that the government should have a budget surplus to dampen inflationary pressures and to achieve a balanced budget over a longer time horizon.

The federal government and many economists have used Keynes's economic theories to justify perpetual government budget deficits. Keynes proposed public spending programs and temporary government budget deficits during the exceptional circumstances of the Great Depression when unemployment rates were unusually high. Keynes's economic theories are now used to justify budget deficits whenever an economy is operating below its loosely-defined "full potential capacity." Many scholars believe that he would surely be opposed to the continual large budget deficits that the US, Japan, and other countries have relied on in an attempt to stimulate economic growth in recent decades.

Keynes also believed that gold could serve as a linchpin for sound money. In a speech to European allies in 1943, Keynes said, "It is likely the confidence gold gives can still play a useful part." Keynes headed the British delegation to Bretton Woods while Harry White was the senior American official. Together they designed the Bretton Woods agreement, which established a fixed exchange rate of US $35 per ounce of gold and allowed foreign central banks to exchange US dollars for gold at this rate.

The Austrian School of Economics

The Austrian School of economics is a school of thought that has its roots in late nineteenth-century Vienna with the work of Carl Menger, Eugen Bohm von Bawerk, Friedrich von Wieser, and others. While some aspects of the Austrian School have been incorporated into mainstream economics, it rejects aggregate macroeconomic analysis and econometrics.

In the late twentieth century, a split had developed among those who self-identify with the Austrian School. One group, following Ludwig von Mises and Murray Rothbard, dismisses empirical methods and mathematical models and offers an alternative paradigm to mainstream theory and seeks to promote a political philosophy of individualism. Many of these followers are Americans affiliated with the Mises Institute. A second group, building on the work of Friedrich von Hayek (often called F. A. Hayek), follows the broad framework of mainstream neoclassical economics including mathematical models and is more consistent with a political philosophy of social democracy.

Ludwig von Mises was born in 1881 and received his doctorate in law from the University of Vienna, where he was influenced by Carl Menger and Eugen Bohm von Bawerk. Mises concluded that the only viable economic policy for the human race was a policy of unrestricted laissez-faire, of free markets, and the unhampered exercise of the right of private property, with government strictly limited to the defense of person and property within its territorial area. Mises developed a business cycle theory that blamed depressions on inflationary bank credit encouraged by central banks.

Friedrich von Hayek was born in 1899 and earned doctorates in law and political science at the University of Vienna. Afterwards, he worked for Ludwig von Mises in Vienna on legal and economic issues for the Austrian government. He eventually joined the faculty at the London School of Economics in 1931 and later had teaching stints at the University of Chicago, University of Freiburg, UCLA, and the University of Salzburg. He is probably best known for his book *The Road to Serfdom*, which advocates individualism and classic liberalism (more commonly called libertarianism in the United States).

While some followers of the Austrian school of economics ridicule Keynes, he had a friendly working relationship with F. A. Hayek. When Hayek and the rest of the London School of Economics moved to Cambridge in 1940 to escape the German blitz, Keynes found him rooms to live and work at his college. They remained in contact until Keynes's death in 1946. When Keynes received an early copy of Hayek's book *The Road to Serfdom*, he praised it with some reservation. He wrote to Hayek:

In my opinion it is a grand book. We all have the greatest reason to be grateful to you for saying so well what needs so much to be said. You will not expect me to accept quite all the economic dicta in it. But morally and philosophically I find myself in agreement with virtually the whole of it; and not only in agreement with it, but in a deeply moved agreement.

Hyman Minsky and Financial Instability

Hyman Minsky is an American economist born in 1919. He taught at Brown University, UC Berkeley, and Washington University in St. Louis. After he retired as a professor, he was a distinguished scholar at the Levy Economics Institute, where his numerous articles are archived. He considered himself to be a Keynesian economist and wrote a book *John Maynard Keynes* (1975). However, Minsky was uncomfortable with the way most economists interpreted Keynes. Minsky supported some government intervention in financial markets, opposed the financial deregulation policies of the 1980s, stressed the importance of the Federal Reserve as a lender of last resort, and argued against the excessive accumulation of debt. He also rejected the efficient market hypothesis in favor of what he called the financial instability hypothesis that he developed.

Minsky proposed the financial instability hypothesis to explain the nature of financial cycles and their impact on the business cycle. Minsky argued that during a period of prosperity, investors take more and more risk until lending exceeds what borrowers can pay from incoming revenues. When overindebted investors are forced to sell even their less speculative positions to make good on their loans, financial markets decline and create a severe demand for cash. Minsky did not develop mathematical models to quantify the process. Steven Keen, an Australian economist, has since developed quantitative models to estimate the impact of changes in debt levels on gross domestic product.

Milton Friedman and Monetarism

Milton Friedman is an American economist who was born in 1912. He became a professor of economics at the University of Chicago in 1946 and taught there for thirty years. In 1976, he was awarded the Nobel Prize in economics for his work on "consumption analysis, monetary history and theory, and for his demonstration of the complexity of stabilization policy." He and Anna Schwartz coauthored *Monetary History of the United States, 1867–1960*, which argued that the Great Depression was caused by the Federal Reserve's monetary policies. After his retirement from teaching, he became a senior research fellow at the Hoover Institution at Stanford University.

Friedman was the main proponent of the monetarist school of economics and rejected the use of fiscal policy as a tool of demand management. He was an advocate of the quantity theory of money - the idea that changes in the money supply have a direct, proportional relationship with the price level. He believed that the best solution to the problems of inflation and short-term fluctuations in employment and GNP would be a money supply rule. Central banks should increase the money supply at a constant percentage rate each year, regardless of the stage of the business cycle. In Friedman's book, *The Counter-Revolution in Monetary Theory* (1970), he wrote:

> Inflation is always and everywhere a monetary phenomenon in the sense that it is and can be produced only by a more rapid increase in the quantity of money than in output.... A steady rate of monetary growth at a moderate level can provide a framework under which a country can have little inflation and much growth. It will not produce perfect stability... but it can make an important contribution to a stable economic society.

Monetary Inflationism

Few economists would identify themselves as *inflationists*. The term is often used to condemn economists who promote large fiscal deficits and/or high rates of money supply growth in order to achieve a higher level of inflation, low rate of unemployment, or some other economic benefit.

Central banks are wary of deflation because debt becomes more difficult to service as interest and principal obligations are usually stated in nominal terms. If there is already a high debt level in the economy, deflation will result in higher default rates and a credit contraction.

Inflation is a means of reducing the debt load. Some consider a high level of inflation to be a broad-based de facto debt restructuring as it transfers wealth from creditors to debtors. While inflation will tend to lower default rates, the purchasing power of the money received by creditors will be lower.

Part of the rationale for monetary inflationism is that central bank purchases of financial assets raises the price level of bonds and common stocks. This "wealth effect" encourages households to increase consumption of goods and services. Economists have different opinions regarding the wealth effect. For instance, David Backus finds no evidence that the dot-com bubble of the late 1990s and the subsequent bust had any significant impact on household consumption. However, economists Carroll and Zhou estimate that household consumption increased by 6% for every dollar increase in home equity value.

Ben Bernanke, who served as chairman of the Federal Reserve from 2006 to 2014, has been one of the most active proponents of monetary inflationism. From 2008 to 2015, the monetary base (consisting of coins, Federal Reserve notes, and Federal Reserve Bank credit, which are deposits by commercial banks at Federal Reserve Banks) increased nearly fivefold to a current level exceeding $4 trillion. There was a corresponding increase in the size of the Federal Reserve balance sheet without any significant increase in capital, arguably bringing the Federal Reserve close to a state of insolvency. Since Janet Yellen became chairman of the Federal Reserve in January 2014, the high level of the monetary base and low capital ratio of the Federal Reserve have been maintained.

Stephen Williamson, a research economist at the Federal Reserve Bank of St. Louis, reviewed the economic literature and wrote a review essay regarding financial crises and central bank policy.

> Evidence in support of Bernanke's view of the channels through which QE works is at best mixed.... Further, there is no work, to my knowledge, that establishes a link from QE to the ultimate goals of the Fed—inflation and real economic activity. Indeed, casual evidence suggests that QE has been ineffective in increasing inflation. For example, in spite of massive central bank asset purchases in the U.S., the Fed is currently falling short of its 2% inflation target. Further, Switzerland and Japan, which have balance sheets that are much larger than that of the U.S., relative to GDP, have been experiencing very low inflation or deflation.

Ben Bernanke has cited the work of Milton Friedman and Anna Schwartz to justify the Fed's policy of monetary inflation. During a speech on Milton Friedman's birthday in November 2002, Bernanke said, "I would like to say to Milton and Anna: Regarding the Great Depression. You're right, we (the Fed) did it. We're very sorry. But thanks to you, we won't do it again."

In an opinion published by the *Wall Street Journal* in July 2009, Anna Schwartz was highly critical of Ben Bernanke and stated that he did not deserve reappointment as Federal Reserve Chairman due to "sins of commission and omission." She wrote:

Mr. Bernanke seems to know only two amounts: zero and trillions. Before 2008 there were only moderate increases in the Federal Reserve's aggregate balance sheet numbers, but since then the balance sheet has exploded by trillions of dollars. The increase was spurred by the Fed's loans to troubled institutions and purchases of securities.

Why is easy monetary policy such a sin? Because in such an environment, loans are cheap and borrowers can finance every project that they dream up. This results in excesses, and also increases the severity of the recession that inevitably follows when the bubble bursts.

Conclusion

Generally, higher debt levels relative to income lead to higher default rates that result in a contraction of credit availability. The credit cycle has an impact on economic growth. Although governments often adopt policies such as large budget deficits to avoid credit and economic contraction, their efforts appear to be futile in the long run. Governments may actually cause bigger swings in credit and economic cycles by artificially stimulating credit growth and asset prices.

References

"Bretton Woods System." Iowa State University Department of Economics blog. http://www2.econ.iastate.edu/classes/econ355/choi/bre.htm

Caplan, Bryan. "Why I Am Not an Austrian Economist." George Mason University, Department of Economics. http://econfaculty.gmu.edu/bcaplan/whyaust.htm

Hoppe, Hans-Hermann. "Why Mises (and not Hayek)?" Mises Daily Blog. October 10, 2011. https://mises.org/library/why-mises-and-not-hayek

Hyman P. Minsky biographical profile. Levy Economics Institute of Bard College. http://www.levyinstitute.org/about/minsky/

"Keynes and Hayek—Prophets for Today." *The Economist*. March 14, 2014. http://www.economist.com/blogs/freeexchange/2014/03/keynes-and-hayek

"Profiles—Ludwig von Mises." Mises Institute website. https://mises.org/profile/ludwig-von-mises

Reuss, Alejandro. "*The General Theory* and the Current Crisis: A Primer on Keynes' Economics." Dollars & Sense—Real World Economics blog. http://www.dollarsandsense.org/archives/2009/0509reusskeynesintro.html

Schwartz, Anna Jacobson. "Man without a Plan." *New York Times* Opinion. July 26, 2009. http://www.nytimes.com/2009/07/26/opinion/26schwartz.html?_r=1&pagewanted=print

Stanfield, J. B. "Adam Smith on Education." Newcastle University, E. G. West Centre blog, March 11, 2005. http://egwestcentre.com/2005/03/11/adam-smith-on-education/

The Concise Encyclopedia of Economics. http://www.econlib.org/library/Enc/bios

Wapshott, Nicholas. *Keynes Hayek—The Clash That Defined Modern Economics*. W. W. Norton & Company, Inc., 2011.

Wikipedia. https://en.wikipedia.org

Williamson, Stephen D. "Current Federal Reserve Policy under the Lens of Economic History: A Review Essay." Federal Reserve Bank of St. Louis, Research Division. Working Paper 2015-015A. http://research.stlouisfed.org/wp/2015/2015-015.pdf

CHAPTER 14

Portfolio Allocation

Never bet on the end of the world. It only happens once.

—Art Cashin, director at
UBS Financial Services Inc.

Efficient Portfolios

Harry Markowitz developed the concept of the efficient frontier, which is defined as the combination of securities portfolios or asset classes that maximize expected return for any level of expected risk as measured by standard deviation of the portfolio.

There are a few points to be made about calculating the efficient frontier. First, we can only know if a portfolio is efficient after the fact because our assumptions will deviate from the unknowable future. Second, many people will be uncomfortable with portfolios on the efficient frontier because they are usually not broadly diversified. An asset class that has had high returns recently will often receive a large portfolio weighting while other asset classes receive zero weighting. This can be overcome in some software programs by establishing constraints—minimum and maximum weights for various asset classes. The use of constraints will result in portfolios that are suboptimal compared to the efficient frontier, but they will be more broadly diversified.

In spite of the difficulty of establishing good forecasts for return, volatility, and correlation coefficients for various asset classes, estimating the efficient frontier is a useful exercise. If we are using reasonable assumptions for the future, it increases the likelihood of achieving a better trade-off between return and risk.

Correlation Matrix

Correlation coefficients are statistical measures of the relationship between two variables. There are several correlation coefficients, but the most commonly used for investment purposes is the Pearson correlation coefficient, which has a range of values between +1 and –1. If the Pearson correlation coefficient is +1, there is a perfect positive linear relationship between the two variables. If it is –1, there is a perfect negative linear relationship between the two variables. If the coefficient is zero, there is no relationship.

Some investment information sources use historical returns to compute the correlation coefficients between asset classes and/or individual securities. This information is important because a portfolio of investments with returns that have low correlation with each other should be less volatile overall. Portfolios that have investments with highly correlated returns will be more volatile.

A correlation matrix is often displayed in a table that shows all of the correlations between the various asset classes. One website that publishes an asset correlation matrix is www.AssetCorrelation.com. At the bottom of its matrix are different time periods. If you change the time periods, you will see that there are significant changes in the correlation coefficients. They do not remain constant.

Portfolio Analysis Tools

There are websites that provide portfolio analysis tools that are free or reasonably priced. Morningstar.com has screens for mutual funds and stocks. Its Morningstar.com premium service has additional tools available for a reasonable cost. Its portfolio "X-Ray" reports show the portfolio breakdown by asset class, a stock style box (value, core or growth, and capitalization), stock sector, stock type, stock statistics, fees and expenses, world regions, and bond style.

Morningstar Office is a service used by investment professionals at a higher cost, which has some analytical tools that go beyond the Morningstar.com premium service. It is possible to change various market assumptions regarding returns, volatility, and correlation coefficients for various asset classes to compare the efficiency of various portfolio allocations. If you are working with an advisor who has Morningstar Office or similar tools available, they should be able to respond to questions regarding the efficiency of your portfolio.

PortfolioVisualizer.com has a website that includes the following: (1) asset correlations, (2) efficient frontier, (3) Monte Carlo simulation, (4) timing models, (5) factor analysis, and (6) portfolio backtest. Free registration on the website allows users to save portfolios and models for continuing work in the future. The efficient frontier analysis on this website is based upon historical returns for selected time periods. It does not allow an investor to input their own assumptions about the future. The efficient frontier is not static, and the efficient portfolio mix will change depending on the historical period selected.

Research Affiliates publishes on a monthly basis their real (after inflation) ten-year expected risk and return forecasts for a variety of asset classes. Navigation tabs allow users to access more detailed information on core asset classes or to explore specific asset classes. There is no cost for the information available on their website. More than $150 billion in assets are managed worldwide using investment strategies developed by Research Affiliates.

Conclusion

Investors should have some variety in their investment portfolios. If the assets that are chosen have a low correlation with each other, the expected volatility of the portfolios will be reduced. Several website services are available that have information regarding asset class correlation, expected returns, volatility, and portfolio efficiency.

References

Asset Correlation.com—major assets: http://www.assetcorrelation. com/majors

Khan, Samir. "Correlation Matrix—Guide and Spreadsheet for Investors. http://investexcel.net/correlation-matrix-excel-vba/

Morningstar. www.morningstar.com

Portfolio Visualizer. www.portfoliovisualizer.com

Research Affiliates. http://www.researchaffiliates.com/assetalloca- tion/Pages/Core-Overview.aspx

Wikipedia. www.wikipedia.com

CHAPTER 15

Fund and Advisor Considerations

> Superior investors make more money in good times than they give back in bad times.
> —Howard Marks,
> cofounder of Oaktree Capital Management

Why Investment Funds?

Mutual funds, ETFs, and closed-end funds offer investors a means of obtaining diversification in their investment portfolios while keeping transaction costs low. Typically, if an investor wishes to select individual stocks or bonds, he would have to invest a minimum of $100,000 to obtain an adequate level of diversification while keeping transactions costs reasonably low. This can be accomplished with less capital in an investment fund because of the diversification of the various securities in the fund's portfolio.

Investors in mutual funds, ETFs, and closed-end funds also benefit from professional management. The best investment managers often beat their benchmark by small margins, but when these marginal effects are compounded over several years, there can be a substantial difference in results.

Mutual Fund Information Sources

There are a number of good sources of information on mutual funds, ETFs, and closed-end funds. Morningstar (www.morningstar.com) provides information on mutual funds, ETFs, closed-end funds, and individual stocks. The company rates mutual funds, ETFs and closed-end funds with a star rating range of one to five, with five being the highest performance rating. 10% of funds within a category receive a five-star rating and 10% of funds receive a one-star rating based upon risk and load-adjusted performance over the past three-, five-, and ten-year periods. Funds that have not been evaluated or have less than three years of history are not rated.

In contrast to its backward-looking star rating, Morningstar also has a forward-looking medal rating of funds. An analyst rating is based upon the analyst's conviction in the fund's ability to outperform its peer group and/or relevant benchmark on a risk-adjusted basis over the long-term. The analyst rating is based upon five pillars: process, performance, people, parent, and price. If a fund receives a positive rating of gold, silver, or bronze, Morningstar analysts expect the fund to outperform its peer group and/or benchmarks over a full market cycle of at least five years. Neutral or negative ratings may also be assigned to funds. Some funds have not been fully evaluated by Morningstar and have no medal ratings.

Morningstar offers much of their information to the general public for free. The company also offers a reasonably priced premium subscription service that includes additional services, such as analyst opinions, premium stock and fund screeners, and portfolio X-ray reports to evaluate overall asset allocation, sector weights, geographic distribution, duration, and credit quality of an investment portfolio.

Closed-End Fund Information Sources

The Closed-End Fund Association (CEFA) is a national trade association that represents the closed-end fund industry. Their website (www.cefa.com) has free information on a variety of closed-end funds and features such as a portfolio tracker and fund screener. There are insightful articles and conference call replays. It's an excellent resource for investors who have an interest in closed-end funds.

A second free source of information on closed-end funds is CEF Connect (www.CEFconnect.com), a site sponsored by Nuveen Investments, Inc., with data provided by Morningstar. The site has portfolio tracker and fund screener capabilities, as well as an education center.

Operating Expenses

The various types of funds have management and other related operating expenses. Some of the index funds have annual operating expenses of only 10 basis points (0.10%) or even lower. Factor funds or actively managed funds have fund operating expenses that typically range between 30 basis points (0.30%) and 100 basis points (1.00%).

Unrealized Appreciation and Depreciation

The statement of assets and liabilities of a fund will have a section that lists the components of net assets or shareholders' equity. One of the items listed will be net unrealized appreciation or depreciation. The net asset value calculation of an investment fund generally does not include any accrued tax liability for unrealized gains or an accrued benefit for unrealized losses.

If a fund has net unrealized appreciation, the fund may have some realized gains that are associated with purchases from earlier years. This may create an additional tax burden for more recent shareholders.

If a fund has net unrealized depreciation, a portion of future distributions may not be taxable. If a portion of the losses are realized, they can be used to offset realized gains in the current year or carried over to future years. During a bear market, there are often many funds with unrealized losses or capital loss carryovers.

Advantages of Institutional Investors

In addition to the advantage of efficient diversification, institutional investors may have some other advantages over an individual investor. Trading costs as a percentage of the assets may be lower due to the use of better information systems, the availability of peer-to-peer trading systems, and algorithmic trading. Bond traders normally receive better pricing in the secondary market if they are able to place orders in larger quantities.

Some fixed-income securities are complex instruments: mortgage-backed securities, collateralized loan obligations, and asset-backed securities, for example. In order to properly evaluate them, information sources such as a Bloomberg terminal are required that are not normally available to individual investors.

Securities Lending

Some investment companies and publications have discussed the benefit of securities lending by managed funds to earn some incremental income. Institutional investors can lend securities that are owned by a mutual fund, ETF, or closed-end fund to those that want to sell short those securities. Lending of securities must be authorized by the fund's organizing documents and be disclosed in its prospectus. If securities are lent out, the fund must receive collateral with a value that equals or exceeds the value of the securities lent. The lender of securities may receive some fee for the arrangement in addition to the income earned on the collateral.

The Investment Company Institute reviewed the 500 largest US long-term funds and found that only 37.6% of the 500 funds lent securities, and of those that did, fewer than one in five lent more than 5% of their assets. For the vast majority of funds, securities lending is not a material consideration.

Institutional Class Shares

Independent financial advisors usually have access to institutional class shares that have lower operating expenses and no sales charges or 12b-1 fees (deferred commissions). The operating expense ratio of institutional class shares is typically 30 to 40 basis points lower than no-load retail class shares of the same fund. The use of institutional class shares will lower the total cost of management if an investor is working with an advisor that uses them.

Brokerage firms usually offer only share classes that have a sales commission at the time of purchase and/or 12b-1 deferred sales charges. They may offer institutional class shares for large accounts that meet a certain minimum order size.

Sustainable, Responsible, and Impact Investing

Sustainable, responsible, and impact (SRI) investing strategies have grown in recent years. The US SIF Foundation estimates that total US-domiciled assets under management using SRI strategies were at $6.57 trillion at the start of 2014, or 18% of assets under professional management.

A variety of criteria are used to meet SRI objectives. Generally, SRI investors want investments in corporations that promote environmental stewardship, consumer protection, good labor relations, human rights, and diversity. They may want to exclude companies involved in alcohol, animal welfare violations, tobacco, unhealthy food, gambling, pornography, weapons, contraception, abortion, and fossil fuel production. US SIF Foundation currently tracks 206 mutual funds that employ SRI strategies. Investors may review financial performance, proxy voting, screening and advocacy criteria of the funds on the US SIF website at: http://charts.ussif.org/mfpc/.

Impact investing is considered a more proactive approach, where investments are made with the intention of generating beneficial social or environmental impact alongside a financial return. Many impact investments are private equity or venture capital investments.

Total Cost of Management

The total cost of management will include both the management fees of the investment companies that manage the individual securities and the management fee of a financial advisor or commissions of a broker that selects or recommends the investment funds.

If closed-end funds are included in an investment portfolio, investors should consider the additional income received due to funds trading at a discount to net asset value. In some cases, this additional income may even exceed the operating expenses of the fund.

Robo-Advisors

Investors may want to consider a "robo-advisor," especially for smaller accounts that may otherwise have a management fee that is high relative to the account value. Robo-advisors offer reduced management fees that are typically one-quarter to one-half of a traditional advisor's fee but offer little or no personalized service. Investors complete a questionnaire online regarding investment goals, risk tolerance, expected retirement, and withdrawal plans. On the basis of the questionnaire, one of several model portfolios is designated for the account. The end result may be similar to what a traditional advisor would recommend but without the personal touch.

Human Advisors

There is a broad range of services and fee schedules for financial advisors. An investor who is considering a registered investment advisor should read the advisor's disclosure document (Form ADV) carefully and be comfortable with an advisor's process for managing investment portfolios as well as their fee schedule.

Conclusion

The use of investments such as mutual funds, ETFs, and closed-end funds are an efficient way to achieve broad diversification. Investors have resources available to select their own investment funds and may want to consider sustainable, responsible, and impact investment strategies. Unrealized appreciation and/or depreciation of investment funds can have significant tax implications for distributions to taxable investors.

There has been a trend in the investment management industry to reduce management fees for both funds and financial advisors. The use of institutional class mutual fund shares by an advisor will lower fund operating expenses that are charged to investors. Investors should carefully review a registered investment advisor's Form ADV and the total cost of management of their investment portfolio.

References

Closed-End Fund Association. www.cefa.com

CEF Connect. www.cefconnect.com

Grohowski, Bob. "Securities Lending by Mutual Funds, ETFs, and Closed-End Funds: The Basics." Investment Company Institute Viewpoints. September 15, 2014 https://www.ici.org/viewpoints/view_14_sec_lending_01

Morningstar. www.morningstar.com

"Report on US Sustainable, Responsible and Impact Investing Trends 2014." US SIF Foundation. http://www.ussif.org/Files/Publications/SIF_Trends_14.F.ES.pdf

US SIF Foundation:the Forum for Sustainable and Responsible Investment. http://www.ussif.org/index.asp

ABOUT THE AUTHOR

Robert G. Kahl, CFA, CPA, MBA is a Chartered Financial Analyst ® charter holder, Certified Public Accountant, and has an MBA degree from UC Berkeley. He has over 20 years of experience in the investment management industry and more than 10 years of experience in accounting and corporate financial planning and analysis. He is the managing member of Sabino Investment Management, LLC. Websites for more information are: www.bobkahlcfa.com and www.sabinoim.com

CPSIA information can be obtained
at www.ICGtesting.com
Printed in the USA
FSOW03n0038260517
34462FS

9 781684 092680